# 101

## BOARDROOM PROBLEMS
### AND HOW TO SOLVE THEM

# BOARDROOM
# PROBLEMS
## AND HOW TO SOLVE THEM

ELI MINA

**AMACOM**

**AMERICAN MANAGEMENT ASSOCIATION**

New York • Atlanta • Brussels • Chicago • Mexico City • San Francisco
Shanghai • Tokyo • Toronto • Washington, D.C.

Special discounts on bulk quantities of AMACOM books are
available to corporations, professional associations, and other
organizations. For details, contact Special Sales Department,
AMACOM, a division of American Management Association,
1601 Broadway, New York, NY 10019.
Tel.: 212-903-8316 Fax: 212-903-8083
E-mail: specialsls@amanet.org
Website: www.amacombooks.org/go/specialsales
To view all AMACOM titles go to: www.amacombooks.org

Library of Congress Cataloging-in-Publication Data

Mina, Eli.
    101 boardroom problems and how to solve them / Eli Mina.
        p.    cm.
    Includes bibliographical references and index.
    ISBN-13: 978-0-8144-1058-5
    ISBN-10: 0-8144-1058-8
        1. Boards of directors.    2. Strategic planning.    3. Group decision making.
    I. Title.    II. Title: One hundred and one boardroom problems and how to solve them.

HD2745.M56 2009
658.4'22—dc22

                                                                      2008021541

Printing Number

10   9   8   7   6   5   4   3   2   1

*I dedicate this book to
the memory of my beloved parents,*
SARA AND MEIR MINA,
*who instilled in me the discipline, principles,
and values that are at the core of this book.*

# C O N T E N T S

# FOREWORD

This is not a book you are holding in your hand.

It is magic.

If you have gotten as far as this Foreword, you are probably already involved with a Board or an organization. You may have a specific problem, you may be at your wits' end because of one or more dysfunctional Board members, or you may just be interested in how you can make your Board more effective, your meetings more positive, and your decisions more balanced and sensible.

Whatever the reason, you have come to the right place. *101 Boardroom Problems and How to Solve Them* is a readable, practical look at 101 Board dysfunctions—and how to solve them. Author Eli Mina's insightful and easy to understand analyses make Board development a game that anyone can play—and win.

I first met Eli Mina in 2003, when the leadership of the American Library Association was looking for a replacement parliamentarian to advise us on meetings, rules of order, and shared decision making. It may come as a surprise, but the 125-year-old ALA may arguably be one of the most complex organizations in existence. The organization has 66,000 national and international members, a thirteen-member Board, a policy-making council of more than 180 members, and eleven divisions with their own Boards. It also has approximately 1,000 committees and subcommittees (they change constantly so no one can be absolutely sure how many exist at any one point) and about 5,000 committee members.

Until 2003, the association faced many challenges and problems. The three-day council meetings were often fractious and bogged down in parliamentary maneuvering, the Board had a reputation for contentiousness, committees often worked at cross-purposes, and the organization had gone through a series of executive directors. The association continued to do important work, but perceptions of its governance were not always positive.

Then Eli Mina entered the picture. Eli may be the most soft-spoken person you will ever meet. People often have to crane forward to catch what he is saying. What they hear when they do is a dramatically different approach to group decision making—one that focuses on the best decisions, informed by the best thinking of all, supported by those involved, driven by mission and strategies, and energizing the organization. Procedures and rules of order are just part of this new approach to more effective organizational decision making.

Today, the situation at ALA is dramatically different from the way it was before Eli came to us in 2003. Council meetings are now both pleasant and well focused, and the new air of civility is widely commented on. The Board, which had already been working on a formal development program when Eli arrived, has been receiving favorable comments on its decisions and improved communications. Division Boards and committee chairs are being trained on how to conduct effective meetings. A series of web podcasts are in place for use by members who cannot attend face-to-face training.

The association continues to wrestle with important and sometimes contentious policy decisions, and members continue to differ on how best to meet the challenges facing a national and international organization in today's complex and changing society. The difference now is an understanding of the importance of the decision-making process and experience in building a democracy that is inclusive and engaging while also being effective and efficient. Positive comments about the changed environment are frequent, and it is much easier to find candidates for office.

The good news is that the approach to more effective decision making—and more pleasant and productive meetings—does not require the ongoing involvement of a consultant. Eli's approach will give your Board the tools it needs to examine its own workings and culture and to begin moving to a more productive and satisfying world of decision making.

As you read in this book about the 101 dysfunctions, you will probably see yourself and others reflected in the examples. Eli has an enormous base of experience and has seen Board behaviors that would make a normal person cringe. Reading his examples will help your Board better understand its own behaviors. This self-examination is the first step toward building better decision-making teams, ones that increase opportunities and reduce risks for your organization.

So sit back and enjoy what might be the most entertaining— and useful—book ever written about Board development.

**Keith Michael Fiels**
*Executive Director, American Library Association*
May 2008

# INTRODUCTION

Before becoming a consultant on meetings and effective decision making, I was employed as an engineer. My motto then was: *Silence is golden*. Keeping quiet in meetings was safe and risk-free, and rarely did anyone solicit my ideas anyway. Had I shared my input, however, it might have improved the quality of my team's decisions and reduced its mistakes. Silence is a common and highly damaging Boardroom problem, one that increases risk and diminishes opportunities.

In 1984, I launched my consulting practice on meetings and rules of order. I had fun advising Boards on demystifying the rules of order and using them sensibly and intelligently to facilitate progress while protecting basic rights. While doing this work, I discovered another Boardroom problem: excessive reliance on rules of order. Boards become entangled in motions, amendments, and other formal procedures and are thereby distracted from core issues. They lose precious time, and their capacity to make quality decisions is eroded.

Since that time, I've observed Boards and councils—which are entrusted to govern substantial organizations and oversee significant mandates and large budgets—do the following: act impulsively, amateurishly, and childishly; display no strength in the face of vocal minorities; place narrow interests ahead of community interests; show no ability to tolerate differences of opinion or benefit from them; and invent solutions without first defining the problems.

What makes Boardroom problems especially puzzling is the fact that, as individuals, many Board members are educated, accomplished, and highly dedicated to their organizations. Some are prominent and respected community leaders. But put them together in a setting where they must share decision-making powers with others, and you often get trouble.

Why do so many Boards become mildly, moderately, or even

severely dysfunctional? Do Boardroom problems indicate malice and a deliberate disregard for the organization or the community that the Board is mandated to serve? I think not.

Consider this thought: *Never attribute to malice what can be attributed to misunderstandings, a lack of knowledge, or systemic weaknesses.* Even if you are certain that someone is acting maliciously, it is more productive to examine the systemic deficiencies that may be the root causes of a specific Boardroom problem. Only then can lasting solutions be found.

## KEY PRINCIPLES AND DEFINITIONS

As the governing body of an organization or community, a Board has the duty to provide proactive, mature, sophisticated, and trustworthy leadership. Board decision making is shared among the members, usually on the basis of one-member–one-vote.

The functioning of Boards requires substantial investments in meetings, travel, staff support, liability insurance, and so on. Given this investment, Board decision making should yield higher returns than the quicker and less costly unilateral decision making, whereby one leader makes the decisions, with or without consulting others. Indeed, when a Board is effective, the above investments yield quality decisions and effective stewardship. In such cases, the Board is an asset. On the other hand, if a Board is mediocre or dysfunctional, the return on investment is small or nonexistent.

When a Board becomes a liability, or when its action or inaction impedes progress, it can be argued that the organization might be better off without a Board altogether. Some might even suggest that in such cases, more could be accomplished under the unilateral stewardship of a competent, honest, and principled administrator.

## THE PROCESS AND SUBSTANCE OF BOARD DECISION MAKING

The success of a Board is determined by both the substance of its decisions and the manner in which they are made. An effective

Board *generates quality decisions, together, and within a reasonable amount of time.* Such a Board balances the need for effectiveness and efficiency with the need to engage its members as equal partners in debate and shared decision making.

It should be noted that *process* (the manner in which a decision is made) is just as important as *substance* (the decision itself). A substantively good decision may fail because it was rushed, minorities were bullied, or the community and stakeholders were not sufficiently informed or consulted.

Below are five *substantive* criteria and five *process* criteria for Board decision making. You may use them to score your Board's decisions and processes. Allocate up to 10 points for each criterion, with 10 representing full satisfaction, and then add the scores. If your Board is functioning well, the grand total for both sets of criteria will be between 70 and 100 points.

Starting with the five *substantive* criteria, a Board decision should be:

1. *Strategic.* The decision supports the attainment of the organization's mission, vision, and strategic goals. It transcends short-term crises and narrow issues and addresses broad and long-term priorities.

2. *Informed.* The decision is based on knowledge and objective analysis of benefits versus risks. It is not tainted by anger, envy, narrow interests, premeeting promises, conflicts of interest, and so on.

3. *Smart.* The decision employs creativity and innovation. It seeks to optimize the use of human, financial, and other resources and maximize the benefits over time.

4. *Balanced and Fair.* The decision achieves an appropriate balance among the needs of the whole organization, the needs of individuals and constituent units, and any other legitimate needs.

5. *Sustainable, Affordable, and Legal.* The decision is realistic and can be implemented with available and reasonably

foreseen means. It complies with legal requirements, bylaws, and policies.

From a *process* perspective, the manner in which a Board decision is made should be:

1. *Collectively Driven*. All Board members are included in the decision-making process, thereby arriving at the same outcome together as active partners and not as acquiescent or reluctant followers.

2. *Transparent and Accountable*. The community is kept informed from the conception of the decision to its implementation. If the decision has substantial impacts, the Board seeks community input on it.

3. *Respectful and Honest*. All parties to decision making are treated with respect and honesty. There are no hidden agendas. The process is not tainted by bullying and trickery.

4. *Measured and Gradual*. The pace of decision making is comfortable. It is neither rushed nor slow. Progress is deliberate and measured. Sufficient time is allocated to the scrutiny of proposals.

5. *Efficient and Timely*. The decision is reached within a reasonable amount of time and without unnecessary delays, which may be caused by a focus on minutiae and by poorly managed meetings.

## BOARDROOM PROBLEMS DEFINED

Given that the function of a Board is to generate quality decisions, together, and in a reasonable amount of time, a Boardroom problem (or dysfunction) is anything that diminishes the Board's ability to function in this manner. Specifically, *a Boardroom problem is an individual behavior or systemic condition that diminishes the substantive quality of a Board decision and/or damages the decision-making process itself.*

Boardroom problems are costly in both tangible and intangible terms. They lead to bad decisions that diminish opportunities and increase risk. They generate internal feuds that can tear apart a highly relevant organization. They sometimes lead to expensive litigation, thereby diminishing the financial and human resources available for core activities. They can build a toxic culture, which makes it hard to attract and retain capable Board members and staff.

It should be noted that a degree of dysfunction is normal. Just like human bodies tolerate the occasional aches and pains or even chronic ailments, so do decision-making bodies. As with problems involving human bodies, measures to address Boardroom problems should be proportionate to their severity: You would not prescribe major surgery when an aspirin would do or when the body would heal itself over time. The same rationale applies to Boardroom problems.

## OBVIOUS AND LESS OBVIOUS PROBLEMS

Not all Boardroom problems are obvious. Some are hidden; that is, they are not obvious at first but flare up later. Others are ingrained in the way the Board operates but remain dormant unless or until something changes and they rise suddenly to the surface. There are also problems that are not really problems at all; they are only perceived as such. Here are some examples of the different types of problems:

- *An Obvious Problem.* Board members are argumentative, interrupt one another, and don't listen to other views. As a result, meetings run late and no closure is achieved, especially on contentious issues. It is obvious that the Board is neither effective nor efficient.

- *A Hidden Problem.* Board members are quiet and very cooperative, and decisions are made quickly. Members are pleased with how fast things get done. Everything seems to be working smoothly. However, at a subsequent meeting, a flawed decision comes back to haunt the Board. It then becomes clear that in its haste to end the earlier meeting, the Board ignored crucial data and made a bad decision.

- *A Dormant Problem*. Poorly written bylaws, ignored in times of harmony, can wreak havoc when controversy erupts. For example, suppose the bylaws of a nonprofit organization do not require Board approval of new membership applications. A hostile takeover is initiated at a membership meeting, and new members who have just joined dictate the outcome.

- *A Perceived Problem*. A new Board member asks tough questions and raises concerns. This slows things down and causes resentment among long-standing members, who had been treating the Board as a social club. Notwithstanding their negative reactions, the new member's actions are not a problem. In fact, the Board and the organization that it governs should be grateful for the diligence and scrutiny of this new member.

## THE ROOT CAUSES OF BOARDROOM PROBLEMS

When confronted with a Boardroom problem, the usual inclination on the part of members is to search for quick fixes. For example, if a Board member acts as a rebel, attacks Board decisions after they are made, and violates confidentiality, there may be an instinctive desire to remove the person from the Board. Such an intervention may indeed tackle the immediate problem, but unless the root causes are addressed, the same situation may repeat itself at some future time.

To address the root causes of Boardroom problems, you need to shift your focus from problematic personal behaviors to systemic deficiencies that serve as nutrients for such behaviors. The root causes of the rebel problem may be the following systemic deficiencies:

■ *A Lack of a Compelling Sense of Collective Purpose.* For example, there may be no mission, vision, and strategic plan, or—if they exist—they may not be adhered to. As a result, the work of the Board may be mediocre and uninspiring. This lack of a compelling collective drive makes room for individual drives (sometimes misguided) to emerge and dominate.

■ *A Lack of Knowledge and Skill to Make Quality Decisions.* Such a deficiency can shift discussions away from logic, objectivity, and professionalism to emotion and hype. A proposal may win not on its merit but on the passion displayed by its rebel proponent.

■ *A Lack of Mentors and Role Models.* Without principled leaders who effectively act as the organization's conscience and compass, there are no barriers to stop assertive yet misguided members from taking center stage.

■ *A Culture of Entitlement and Self-Interest.* The culture of the Board should promote the interests of the organization as a whole. If the Board is instead immersed in a culture of entitlement and self-interest, members focus on themselves and compete for power and control.

■ *Weak Selection Processes.* For example, Board members may be selected on the basis that no one else is available for the job. They are not advised of the required commitment and of the Board's code of conduct before their nomination or selection.

■ *Weak or Nonexistent Board Orientation or Training Programs.* Such programs would emphasize—among other things—the duties to balance individual initiative with teamwork, keep Board confidentiality, adhere to conflict of interest guidelines, place collective interests ahead of narrow ones, and avoid undermining validly made Board decisions. Without such rules of interaction in place and without them being reinforced and monitored regularly, there is a good likelihood that rebels will violate them.

- *A Lack of Feedback and Evaluation.* Board members may be afraid to confront others and give them honest and constructive feedback on counterproductive behaviors. As a result, they may talk *about* rebels instead of talking *to* them. In addition, there may be no regular evaluations of Board members, the Board Chair, the Board as a whole, and the CEO.

- *A Lack of Trust and Respect for the Board from the Community That It Serves.* Such a deficiency tends to generate support for dissenting members and fuel their sometimes misguided causes.

- *A lack of protocol for meetings.* People speak whenever they want, and no effort is made to equalize the opportunities to participate. As a result, rebel members can take over.

These and other systemic deficiencies must be addressed proactively. There should be organized efforts to establish a solid foundation for Board decision making. Such efforts will reinforce the Board's immune system and deprive dysfunctions of the nutrients they need to thrive.

## INTERVENTION PRINCIPLES

An intervention is a measure to treat and/or prevent a Boardroom problem. To be effective, an intervention must be proportionate to the scope and severity of the damage that a problem inflicts. Consider one or more of the following options:

- *Wait a while.* If the problem causes only minimal damage, drawing attention to it may cause undesirable side effects. If the Board is generally effective, its decision-making process will likely recover on its own without any intervention. For example, a minor digression from a meeting agenda, although against the rules, may give Board members a much needed mental break and enable them to reenergize and refresh themselves.

- *Intervene mildly.* Refocus the Board with a gentle reminder: *"Members, we need to get back on track."*

- *Intervene more firmly.* If, despite warnings, a member still engages in personal attacks and name calling, say: *"Jack, we need you to focus on the issues and keep this discussion civilized. If you're not able to do that, we may need to ask you to take some time out."*

- *Try a collective intervention.* If a member rolls his eyes while another member is speaking, ask the speaker to pause and then address the group as a whole instead of addressing the impatient individual: *"Members, we need to show respect and listen to one another, even when we do not agree with other people's views. Can we please have your support?"*

- *Intervene off-line.* If the damage can be tolerated for now, it may be effective to speak to the individual privately at a break or after the meeting: *"Jill, I did not want to embarrass you in front of your colleagues, but your questions showed that you could have prepared better for the meeting. Can we count on you to do this next time?"*

- *Take proactive or preventive measures.* To prevent verbal abuse at a contentious meeting, try this opening script: *"Before we carry on, I need to say this: The issues that we're dealing with today are difficult. Many of you are passionate about your views, but I need to remind you to direct your passion at the issues and not at your colleagues. Can you please help me maintain civility and respect at this meeting? Thank you."*

- *Address root causes.* If a member takes a long time to make a point, the root cause may be a concern that his or her point was not understood (in which case you can repeat and confirm the point) or the fact that the person is naturally verbose (in which case you can give him or her feedback or offer training on communicating concisely and briefly).

■ *Try nonverbal interventions.* If a side conversation is distracting for participants, ask everyone to pause, and then look in the direction of the side talkers. The silence will likely compel them to focus on the meeting.

■ *Try shifting from negative to affirmative language.* Instead of saying, *"Stop disrupting the meeting or I'll ask you to leave,"* try: *"In fairness to everyone, we need to hear from only one person at a time. Can we please respect the rules?"*

Chapters 1 to 10 of this book describe 101 boardroom problems, the damage they potentially inflict on Board decision making, and how to solve or prevent them. The book also includes four appendices: a Board Effectiveness Audit, Board Evaluation Tools, Myths and Truths About Rules of Order, and Tools for Meeting Chairs and Participants.

## APPLICATION OF THIS BOOK

This book builds on the notion that Board decision making should work as a partnership among three entities: (1) the *Board* (providing policy direction), (2) *management* (providing the professional expertise and practical grounding for Board decisions), and (3) the *community* that the Board is mandated to serve (providing input on impending Board decisions).

The book will offer you practical ideas to tackle and prevent Boardroom problems. It draws on more than two decades of experience in mentoring Boards and helping them deal effectively with complex and contentious issues. With this book, your Board will be better positioned to make quality decisions—inclusively, transparently, and efficiently. With it, you will be better able to provide the caliber of leadership that your organization or community deserves.

The material in this book will benefit the following partners in Board decision making:

- Boards as collective entities
- Individual Board members
- Board Chairs, mayors, presidents, or other chief elected officers
- Chief executive officers, executive directors, or those who hold equivalent titles
- Senior professional staff and external advisers to Boards
- Consultants on Board governance and shared decision making
- Community members who want quality leadership from their Boards

It should be noted that:

- The reference to *Board* is interchangeable with the terms *council*, *commission*, or any other title of a governing body or decision-making team.
- Although this book focuses primarily on Boards and other governing bodies, it also applies to committees, task forces, and any groups that make their decisions jointly. Some of it may even apply to staff meetings where decisions are made unilaterally by a manager after hearing from the participants.
- For illustration, some examples in the book refer to male or female Board members. This does not mean that the same problem never involves the opposite gender.

## CAVEATS AND DISCLAIMERS

As you read this book, consider the following caveats and disclaimers:

■ Although the book covers a wide array of Boardroom problems, it is not an all-inclusive panacea for all Board ailments. Your Board may experience its own unique problems, but it can still solve them by utilizing the thought processes that this book provides.

■ This book may surprise or even shock you. It may show the substantial damage inflicted by behaviors that you've considered normal. But there is no need to panic or despair. With a principled approach, you can eradicate bad habits or reduce their negative impacts. You may also wish to consider that a degree of dysfunction is normal and acceptable. Attempts to quickly achieve absolute perfection can create more problems than they solve.

■ Some of the strategies in this book may be hard or impossible to implement under your Board's current realities. To make them work, you may first need to examine systemic deficiencies and reinforce the foundation for decision making, including the Board's direction, governance structure, culture, and other components.

■ Every effort was made in this book to describe Boardroom problems in a generic manner so as to not identify specific organizations. Any resemblances between the problems described in this book and actual situations are purely coincidental.

■ For illustration, each of the 101 problems is described in a specific context, such as that of a corporate, governmental, or nonprofit Board. The dynamics of one type of Board usually apply to others, although the terminology may vary.

■ The information in this book does not constitute legal advice and should not be used as such. I am not a lawyer and cannot advise you on the legal validity (or lack thereof) of the ideas presented. All I can say is that my clients have found these ideas beneficial.

# ACKNOLEDGMENTS

I wish to express my deep gratitude to the individuals who served on the Editorial Board for this book and provided valuable insights, observations, and suggestions. They are:

- Bill Wellburn, Board Chair, Provincial Capital Commission

- Eunice Ludlow, Chief Administrative Officer, Village of Slocan

- Dr. Norman Horrocks, Emeritus Professor, Dalhousie University, Faculty of Management

- Dinny Holroyd, Board Governance Consultant

- Neil Sterritt, Board Governance Consultant

- Stanley French, Executive Director, BC Principals & Vice-Principals Association

Special thanks go to Oren J. Margolis for his assistance in organizing the book and clarifying its various scenarios.

# CHAPTER ONE

# FAULTY DIRECTION

As a governing body, a Board has the duty to establish and maintain a clear and compelling sense of direction. To do so, a Board should develop the following:

- A mission (a statement of why the organization exists)

- A vision (a statement of where the organization is going)

- A strategy (a plan of how the vision will become a reality)

If the above three components are in place and if people across the organization appreciate and support them, there will be fewer problems and—if they occur—the damage they inflict will be limited.

The remainder of this chapter discusses some basic directional problems.

# OUTDATED MISSION

An organization's mission statement was written 150 years ago, and its focus has not been substantially adjusted to reflect current realities and emerging trends. The organization dispenses products and services that are relevant to a shrinking portion of the population. Its leadership is stagnant, embraces the status quo, and has trouble letting go of control and fixed mindsets.

## Potential Damage

The organization may lose its credibility with the broader population. Young people may be reluctant to join the Board. Those who do may be hampered by advocates of the status quo and may eventually lose their enthusiasm and leave. With fewer supporters, the financial base for the organization may shrink. This may make it necessary to increase fees, which—in turn—may cause even more supporters to leave. This chain reaction may lead to the organization's demise.

## Intervention

Express appreciation to long-standing leaders, but suggest that the organization may need a fresh, modern approach. The Board should be reconstituted, keeping some experienced members and adding new ones. The newly constituted Board should then examine the organization's mission openly and with no preconceived ideas, possibly with the assistance of an impartial facilitator. Having revised the mission, vision, and strategic plan, the Board should review them periodically with the CEO to ensure progress.

As previously stated, a mission statement defines why an organization exists. It should address three questions:

1. *Action*: What does the organization do?

2. *Audience*: Whom does the organization serve?

3. *Outcomes*: What results does the organization generate for its audience?

A mission statement should be:

■ Simple, brief, and clear

■ Broad enough to provide flexibility yet sufficiently narrow to create focus

■ Relevant to current realities and anticipative and responsive to emerging trends

■ Meaningful enough to compel support by everyone across the organization

■ Prominently reflected and apparent in all of the organization's activities

PROBLEM

# 2

## OFF-MANDATE ACTIVITIES

The Board of a community services organization is offered the opportunity to organize and oversee a onetime sporting event. The event is an exciting challenge and offers significant financial benefits, but it is outside the organization's core mandate. The Board decides to take on the project and dedicate substantial staff and volunteer resources to it.

### Potential Damage

With resources shifted toward activities that do not advance the organization's mission, less capacity is available for core activities.

Staff and volunteers may wonder: *"Why are we doing this?"* Some may get frustrated and perform at a fraction of their full capacity. Some may even leave, and replacing them may be costly. Finally, if an accident happens as a result of off-mandate activities, there may be liability for the Board collectively or even for its individual members. Such liability may or may not be covered by Directors and Officers insurance.

## Intervention

Bring any off-mandate activities to a swift end. Reassure staff and volunteers that future activities will always be guided by the organization's mission and that the Board will not be seduced by off-mandate projects, even if they seem exciting or financially rewarding. If you are in doubt as to whether a contemplated activity fits within your mandate, consult a lawyer. If it is still desirable to pursue such an activity, modify your legal framework first to permit it.

PROBLEM

3

# VISION BASED ON NEGATIVE ASSUMPTIONS

A Board bases its vision on negative assumptions, envisioning a community that has its own hospital, its own drug rehabilitation and detoxification center, and counselors for abuse victims. The vision has no space for a more positive outlook.

## Potential Damage

Focusing largely on curing illnesses and addictions and recovering from past abuses implies an expectation that these conditions will always exist. With resources being focused on cures, fewer resources are available to develop positive preventive programs, such as education, meaningful employment, and cultural enrichment. Healthy people with positive outlooks will gain nothing from the Board's vision and may end up leaving the community for greener pastures.

## Intervention

Having a mission statement in place, the Board requires a clear vision of an *ideal* future. A vision statement should be distant enough from current reality that it always offers challenge. It also should not be so distant from the current situation that it is impossible to make measurable progress.

With this in mind, you should develop a multiphase vision and strategic plan. A *short-term vision* will focus on the eradication of negative conditions, and a *long-term vision* will focus on building a healthy community, where there will be minimal likelihood of negative conditions. Envision a community where individuals lead fulfilling lives, with plenty of opportunities for education, meaningful employment, comfortable housing, and a culturally and socially rich environment.

## PROBLEM
## 4
## NO STRATEGIC PLANNING

A homeowners' association elects its first Board, which immediately faces a multitude of problems: structural issues with the building, thefts from cars, noise pollution, bylaw violations, and more. The Board is overwhelmed and reacts to the most pressing problems first. But as soon as those are addressed, new ones surface.

In another setting, a Board holds a planning session, which

proves to be very productive. However, at its next meeting, the Board gets preoccupied with immediate crises. Soon, the habit of operating reactively becomes just too hard to break. The strategic plan gathers dust on the shelf. One day the Board will find time for it, but there are more pressing matters now.

## Potential Damage

With efforts focused primarily on immediate crises, long-term priorities receive little or no attention. Board and community members become frustrated by the fact that the organization is driven by external forces and not by a proactively set agenda. Although some community members may tolerate this inferior performance as a fact of life, others may be prompted to take action against the Board or leave. In addition, a Board with no clear direction will find it difficult to resist pressure by special interest groups whose agenda is usually well defined.

## Intervention

With a mission and vision in place, the Board needs to develop a strategic plan to make them a reality. A strategic plan should include specific goals and a schedule of implementation activities. The plan should be divided into manageable components, each of which should be scheduled for discussion at a designated Board meeting.

The documented mission, vision, and strategic plan will be useful only if they are evident in the organization's daily activities. Here are five tips to keep your Board focused on the bigger picture:

1. Schedule a strategic planning session early in the Board's term of office, so the Board can establish short- and long-term goals and priorities. Obtain input from management and the community to improve the plan.

2. Whenever possible, conduct meetings in a way that links agenda items to your mission and vision statements. Discuss at least one strategic priority per meeting and—having discussed it—give appropriate directions to management.

3. Print the mission and vision statements, along with basic meeting rules and code of conduct excerpts, on the backs of name tent cards placed in front of members. This will provide a subtle but constant reminder of the bigger picture.

4. Read the mission statement aloud at the start of each meeting and reinforce it by periodic reminders, as needed.

5. Encourage members to speak up if they believe the Board is off course. For example, they may question how well a certain initiative will advance specific strategic goals and how consistent it is with agreed-upon values and principles.

# CHAPTER TWO

# GOVERNANCE AND STRUCTURAL ISSUES

An organization's governance structure is usually defined by its governing documents, such as the applicable legislation, constitution, bylaws, and articles of incorporation. Structural issues include board size and composition, decision-making powers, jurisdiction, and others.

Structural flaws can be hard to rectify. Bylaw amendments usually require prior notice, a supermajority (e.g., a two-thirds or three-quarters vote), and sometimes also government approval of the filed new bylaws. If structural flaws are entrenched in legislation, changes require action by a legislative assembly.

To be effective, an organizational structure should:

- Be simple, logical, and easy to implement

- Be nimble to enable timely responses to emerging issues

- Impose reasonable restrictions on the powers of the Board and management

- Establish an appropriate balance of power between the Board and the community

- Balance the organization's needs with the needs of its units and members

- Balance the need for continuity on the Board with the need for leadership renewal

This chapter addresses some common problems relating to Board governance and structure.

PROBLEM

# 5

## OVERSIZED BOARD

In an effort to accommodate every constituent unit, the bylaws of a national organization give each unit a seat on the Board. All past presidents are also included on the Board as voting members. As a result, the Board has more than seventy members, spread across a wide geographic area.

### Potential Damage

With so many Board members, travel costs make Board meetings prohibitively expensive and therefore infrequent. Involving Board members as full and equal partners in decision making is a challenge, and most members end up on the sidelines. The large size also makes it difficult for the Board to perform meaningful oversight of the CEO or respond decisively to challenges that require prompt action. Although the Board is technically the governing body, decisions end up being driven by a small committee of Board officers. The result of all of this is that mistrust can develop and factions may form.

## Intervention

Over the immediate term, plan activities to engage all Board members in meaningful debates and consensus building, such as committee and task force work or small breakout groups during meetings. Prior to meetings, use electronic means to engage members in dialogue and consensus building on key issues. At meetings, ensure that formal presentations and reports are kept brief to avoid the lecture-mode that makes it easy for people to tune out. If the above measures are taken, the need to downsize the Board may be reduced.

Over the long term, a form of restructuring may need to be considered to enable the Board to govern effectively and efficiently. You may want to consider instituting two deliberative bodies: (1) a smaller Board that meets regularly, and (2) a large assembly of delegates that meets annually or semiannually. Restructuring options should be considered carefully so the advantages of a larger Board with broader representation are not lost. If such options are to be pursued, prepare the appropriate bylaw amendments in consultation with key stakeholders.

Note that a Board should be large enough to benefit from broadly based input, yet small enough to allow timely progress. A Board size of between six and fourteen members is suggested. Also, terms of office for Board members should be long enough to build experience and continuity, yet short enough to facilitate rotation and renewal and avoid stagnation. In order to force Board renewal, some bylaws limit the number of consecutive Board terms that a person can serve. If term limit bylaws are included, they should be flexible and permit waivers in exceptional cases to avoid the forced loss of members who are at peak performance.

# 6

# OVERCONCENTRATION OF POWERS

Relying on the provisions in its bylaws, the Board of a charity refuses to approve new memberships. As a result, Board members are the only voting members at the charity's annual meeting and reelect themselves or elect their handpicked successors to the Board. The Board thereby retains full control over the charity without accountability to any group outside itself.

## Potential Damage

With so much power held by only a few people, the Board can become arrogant, detached, and nonresponsive to the community that it serves, with no one outside the Board having any real recourse against its actions or inactions. Transparency and accountability are bound to suffer. In time, stakeholder support and donations to the charity may diminish, and the charity's ability to serve its community may therefore be in jeopardy.

## Intervention

Over the short term, a Board with this much power should make extra efforts to be transparent and accountable to its community. Even if not required to do so, it should proactively seek community input before making significant decisions. If transparency and accountability are entrenched, there may be no need to establish a broad voting membership structure.

Over the long term, a broad voting membership structure should be considered for various reasons: to help establish the organization's roots, to dilute the concentration of power and the possibility of any abuse, and to provide recourse for the community if the Board becomes dysfunctional.

# DILUTION OF POWERS

In an organization, the official governing body is the Board, but actual power is spread among local councils, regional blocs, and powerful committees. The bylaws require the Board to consult broadly and extensively and even stipulate that certain decisions must be made jointly or ratified by several decision-making bodies before they take effect.

## Potential Damage

The Board may lose its ability to govern, and the extra decision-making bodies may effectively paralyze the organization. This is especially problematic when such bodies have loosely defined roles, receive no orientation, and have no meaningful accountability. The Board may not be able to enact urgent decisions in a timely manner because it lacks control over the pockets of power. This may increase risk and diminish opportunities for the organization.

## Intervention

In the short term, enhance communication and collaboration between the various bodies and the Board. Work to improve the organization's culture, and emphasize the principle of placing collective interests ahead of narrow interests. Establish a broad-based commitment to helping the organization move forward in a timely fashion despite its complex structure.

Over the long term, the organization's structure and allocation of decision-making powers should be reviewed. This process should balance the need for nimble governance with the need for broad-based democracy, transparency, and accountability. The new structure should be discussed widely before any bylaw amendments are voted on.

PROBLEM

# 8

## ISSUES OF SELF-REGULATION

The Board of a self-regulatory organization is elected by members of a certain profession. The government delegates the Board the authority and duty to protect the public by licensing, setting standards, and regulating and disciplining licensees within the profession. The bylaws stipulate that fees and regulatory bylaws require licensee approval at a general membership meeting.

### Potential Damage

In many situations, it is naive to expect that licensees would be devoid of self-interest and that they would willingly vote to impose economic or administrative hardships on themselves in order to protect the public. This self-regulatory body is required to approve fees at membership meetings, and it may thus find itself unable to increase fees in order to fund the regulatory process in the public interest. Other Boards in similar circumstances may be unable to obtain the membership vote to enact bylaws that are essential for public protection because such bylaws are likely to inconvenience many licensees.

### Intervention

In the short term, you can educate members of the profession about the need to establish high practice standards and to place public interest ahead of their own. Emphasize that self-regulation is a privilege granted by government; and it is not an inherent right. This self-regulation privilege requires the profession to act selflessly and in a manner that the public will respect and trust.

Over the long term, you may wish to seek legislative or bylaw amendments that would place the approval of fee increases and regulatory bylaws in the hands of the Board rather than the general membership. Such amendments should also stipulate that at least a proportion of the Board would consist of public members from outside the regulated profession, so the voice of the public will be heard in the process of Board decision making.

PROBLEM

9

# NO DISCIPLINARY MEASURES

The legislation or bylaws of an organization provide no real method of disciplining a Board member for misconduct. In another setting, disciplinary processes are cumbersome, awkward, and expensive, such as a requirement of court action to remove or penalize a Board member for misconduct.

## Potential Damage

Without effective disciplinary measures, the Board may not be able to meaningfully police itself. Ongoing and unpunished behaviors may convey the message that Board policies need not be taken seriously.

## Intervention

In the short term, take a preventive approach. Clarify guidelines, create a code of conduct, and establish commitment to that code. Select your Board members with diligence, and build a culture so principled that violations will not be contemplated.

Over the long term, you may need to change bylaws or advocate for legislative reform to give the Board greater ability to enforce its policies, as well as the ability to meaningfully and expeditiously punish its members for deliberate and repeated misconduct.

## EMPLOYEES AS BOARD MEMBERS

The bylaws of a particular organization do not prohibit employees from becoming Board members. A manager who is unhappy with the CEO is nominated and elected to the Board. The manager thus becomes both a subordinate to the CEO and a member of the team that supervises the CEO.

### Potential Damage

This situation is awkward for the CEO, who may hesitate to give meaningful supervision to the manager for fear that he will retaliate as a member of the Board.

### Intervention

Explain to the Board the damaging effects of having employees on it, and strongly discourage the practice. Give guidance to the nominating committee to avoid nominating employees to the Board unless the employees have handed in their resignations. If an employee is on the Board, clarify that she must respect the chain of command while functioning as a staff member and must not act in a manner that hampers the CEO in managing the staff.

Over the long term, introduce an appropriate bylaw amendment: *"No employee or contractor for the organization may be nominated, elected, or continue to serve on the Board, and if a Board member becomes an employee or contractor for the organization, such person shall be deemed to have resigned from the Board."*

Some organizations have a policy that requires a two-year cooling-off period before a staff member can become a Board member, and vice versa.

## CHAPTER THREE

# UNETHICAL CULTURE

An organizational culture is the set of norms, expectations, and attitudes that exist across an organization, including its community and Board. A culture is like an unwritten code that compels individual behaviors.

An organizational culture is very powerful. If the community from which a Board is elected has a negative culture—for example, a culture of apathy and acquiescence or a culture of abuse, self-interest, and nepotism—this culture will likely be the Board's culture. On the other hand, if the community has a positive culture, everyone will demand excellence and high performance on the Board. Moreover, a community with a positive culture will not tolerate mediocrity or dysfunctional or unethical behaviors by Board members.

# 11

## CYCLE OF ABUSE

A community elects leaders annually, only to criticize them when they report at the next annual meeting. Innocent errors made by the Board are often interpreted by vocal community members as signs of malice, weakness, or incompetence. Leaders who do what the crowd wants are viewed as friends, and those who don't are abused. Nasty rumors spread fast and poison the air. Trust is a scarce commodity. Successful individuals are envied and undermined.

In another setting, a Board that makes controversial but necessary decisions becomes the target of motions to remove its members before their terms end. Once the members are removed, the new Board members who replaced them realize that it is much easier to criticize from the sidelines than to lead. The new members themselves become the subject of removal motions the following year. The cycle of abuse continues.

### Potential Damage

Serving on the Board becomes a thankless job that effective people will avoid; if such people do join the Board, they may resign after taking too much abuse. When making tough decisions, Board members may be distracted by the fear of offending vocal people or by a desire to please them. In such a culture, adversarial actions (including lawsuits) are likely. Such actions waste time and money and make fewer resources available for positive and much needed initiatives.

### Intervention

Start community-wide discussions about the negative dynamics and how they damage the organization's capacity to serve its constituents. Secure a commitment from everyone to change attitudes and to add a human touch to their interactions. This effort will need to be sustained over a long time as abusive cultures are tough to eradicate.

PROBLEM

# 12

## ACQUIESCENCE AND SUBMISSION

In one community, people do not complain or criticize anything for fear they might offend others or suffer repercussions. When they do speak up, they dilute their comments with apologies. It is considered safer to be quiet and acquiescent, especially when a problem is not seen as such a big deal. People tend to defer to strong leaders or dominant personalities.

### Potential Damage

The culture of the Board, whose members come from the community, is likely to reflect acquiescence and submission. Flawed decisions or disruptive behaviors may therefore go unchallenged. Creative ideas and critical observations may be withheld, which is bound to increase risk and diminish opportunities for the organization.

### Intervention

Convey the message to the Board and the community that input and ideas are valued and appreciated, that people should not hesitate to demand excellence, and that mediocrity should not be tolerated. Publicly recognize and reward individuals for raising points that help the Board reduce risk and increase effectiveness. Finally, encourage everyone to listen openly and nondefensively to make it safe and comfortable for others to speak up.

## PROBLEM
# 13
## CULTURE OF ENTITLEMENT

Individuals in a community believe they are entitled to certain things and must fight those who stand in their way. The good of the community as a whole takes a back seat. People compete intensely for resources and opportunities, and promote their own interests and those of their family members and friends.

In one particular setting where individuals have such sense of entitlement, after an election, the new Board promptly removes the CEO and most staff. The Board then appoints its handpicked friends and family members to fill the vacant positions, with little or no attention to their qualifications. Subsequently, when making decisions, Board members are often driven by a desire to reward friends and return favors. In the next election, an opposing faction wins and acts the same way. Nepotism and corruption have become a way of life.

### Potential Damage

Incompetent staff members may be selected to perform important work, potentially delivering mediocre or poor performance. Effective staff members may be distracted by fear, especially when an election is looming, and may therefore be unable to perform their best. With money and resources used to reward and return favors to friends and family members, less is available to advance the good of the community as a whole. There is no trust and respect for the Board and its decision-making process. A sense of futility and desperation sets in.

### Intervention

Eradicate nepotism, favoritism, and corruption—and do it now! Develop policies that emphasize merit-driven hiring and decision making. Ensure that Board decisions are driven by core values and principles and by a desire to maximize benefits for the community as a whole. Educate the community and lead it away from the culture of entitlement.

## TIPS TO REMEMBER

With everyone expecting excellence and refusing to tolerate mediocrity and unprincipled behaviors, dysfunctions will be detected early and more people will speak up and draw attention to them. To give a boost to your organizational culture, consider the following:

- Educate individuals at all levels on how to identify Boardroom problems, discern their damaging effects, and speak up or intervene appropriately.

- Institute whistle-blowing policies to prevent retribution against those who speak up.

- Recognize and reward individuals for speaking up and drawing attention to problems.

- Institute appropriate penalties against individuals who were aware of problems and did not draw attention to them (especially if damage materialized as a result of their silence).

- Make it safe for people to give feedback. Ensure that all leaders treat feedback as a gift and listen to it intently and nondefensively. Everyone should welcome complaints with the same enthusiasm that they greet compliments.

- Remind everyone that perfection is not a realistic goal and that a degree of dysfunction is normal. Intolerance of Boardroom problems should not become an obsession, and interventions should be proportionate to the damage caused by a problem.

PROBLEM

# 14

# PREOCCUPATION WITH FINANCIAL SELF-INTEREST

Members of an industry association get excited only when their Board proposes initiatives that will likely benefit them and their businesses financially or materially. The most often asked question during annual meetings is: *"What's in it for me and my business?"*

## Potential Damage

When people focus predominantly on their own financial or material results, it is difficult for the Board to take initiatives that provide no such immediate tangible benefits, even when they are the right things to do for the long-term future of the industry. It is a challenge to persuade members to pay higher dues to fund such initiatives. It is even tougher to get their support for initiatives that will provide no tangible benefits in their lifetime but will greatly benefit future generations.

## Intervention

Educate members to expand their outlook from personal gains to community gains, from numeric or tangible results to qualitative or intangible results, and from short-term outcomes to long-term outcomes. Keep in mind that efforts to modify entrenched attitudes and behaviors may require patience, determination, and repetition of key messages. Such efforts may also require a thick skin so that you can withstand the cynicism or even verbal abuse you are likely to receive from critics.

## PROBLEM

# 15

# ADVOCATING CONSTITUENCY INTERESTS

The members of a representational Board are elected or appointed by constituent units, but their duty on the Board is to serve the organization as a whole. Some Board members, however, believe their primary duty is to advocate for and act in the interests of their constituent units. They regularly consult with their units and confirm their wishes before voting at the Board level. Some constituent units even order their Board members to vote a certain way on some issues. Board members who, after listening to debates, vote contrary to the orders of their constituent units are attacked or even disciplined or dismissed when they report back to their units.

## Potential Damage

If members continually advocate for their own units, the Board becomes fractured, with unit representatives pulling in different directions or making deals with others to get a majority for their proposals. In addition, constituent units who order their representatives to vote in a certain way on issues diminish the representatives' ability to truly listen with open minds, learn from the debate, and make informed decisions in the best interests of the organization as a whole. This may taint and bias the process and increase the likelihood of flawed decisions. There is no sense of a coherent and cohesive direction for the organization as a whole.

## Intervention

Advise constituent units that although their Board representatives can be expected to present unit-based input, the duty of the representatives is ultimately to place collective interests ahead of unit interests. Clarify this point for the representatives during Board orientation. Educate units to avoid giving orders to their representatives, as such orders may be unenforceable and are likely to taint and bias the process.

## TIPS TO REMEMBER

To more effectively address the challenge of balancing the interests of constituency units with those of the organization as a whole, consider the following suggestions:

- Upon taking office, Board members should be asked to confirm that they will abide by the principle of placing organizational interests ahead of any other interests.

- Board members should clarify their roles to their constituent units, thereby preventing unfounded expectations at the constituent unit level.

- Prior to Board meetings, Board members should advise their units of upcoming Board issues and seek their input.

- While receiving constituent unit input, Board members should remind local units that local input is merely advisory and that—although Board members will present this input—they must ultimately act in the organization's interests. Board members should discourage local units from attempts to instruct them on how to vote on Board motions.

- At Board meetings, members representing constituent units should provide their local input, as applicable to the discussions.

- Having presented local input, Board members should then switch to learn from the input of their colleagues, the CEO, and professional advisers. As they listen, they should be focusing on broad organizational interests.

■ When it comes to voting, Board members should vote with the organization's interests placed ahead of any other interests, even if their constituent units expressed a strong desire that they vote differently or even ordered them to do so.

■ After Board meetings, members should report back to their constituent units and explain the decisions that were made at the organizational level. Knowing that organizational interests always come first, constituent units should understand and accept the actions of their representatives.

PROBLEM

# 16

# FISHING FOR PARTISAN SUPPORT

A Municipal Council member asks a staff member several leading questions during a public meeting. If the questions are addressed narrowly, the answers will confirm the council member's political position. When the staff member declines to give narrow answers and instead provides proper perspective and a professional response, the council member interrupts and demands yes-or-no answers.

## Potential Damage

Staff members can find themselves in awkward and uncomfortable positions. On the one hand, they want to be helpful and informative. On the other hand, they must limit themselves to providing professional advice without directly supporting or refuting political arguments. As an added damage, citizens who attend council meetings and witness the trickery become cynical of their elected council.

## Intervention

Establish that staff must never be coerced into promoting political positions. Ask council members to appreciate the fact that staff is required to offer *objective* professional advice, untainted by political considerations. Inform staff members that they must be assertive and not hesitate to say: *"With all due respect, I am not here to give political advice. That is not my job. I'm here only to offer my professional expertise. I'll leave the political interpretation to you."*

As a preventive measure, encourage the council to abandon or moderate the focus on partisan politics and become a more cohesive and collaborative decision-making team.

PROBLEM

17

# CONFLICT OF INTEREST

A Board member owns a company that is bidding on a project. He remains present when the Board discusses the project, advocates strongly for his company, and then votes. In fact, his vote tips the scale and gives his company the job. When someone suggests that he may have a conflict of interest (COI), he reacts defensively.

In another setting, after being elected to the council of a homeowners' association, a homeowner presents plans for substantial renovations of her apartment for the council's approval. Before the vote is taken, she is requested to leave because of a conflict of interest and refuses.

## Potential Damage

These are clear COI scenarios, where individuals use their positions as Board members for benefits that they alone receive. The individuals' actions taint the process and make it possible that the decisions will be later challenged and possibly overturned. When the individuals react defensively to suggestions of conflict of interest, it becomes difficult for others to express valid concerns and protect the organization from allegations of bias and corruption.

## Intervention

COI guidelines must be in place to protect the integrity of the decision-making process. Such guidelines should prohibit Board members from using their powers for personal gains unique to themselves. Such guidelines should exclude individuals from debate and from voting if their ability to act independently may be impaired by a COI.

A Board member who has a conflict of interest should take the following steps:

- Disclose the COI to the Board immediately upon becoming aware of it.

- Leave the meeting before the discussion of the issue begins, in order to avoid any possibility of influencing the debate or the vote and in order to avoid making it awkward for other members to speak fully in the discussion.

- Avoid any overt or covert attempt to influence the decision in any way, whether at the meeting or outside the meeting.

- Return to the meeting when the Board proceeds to the next agenda item.

The COI declaration and the absence of the affected Board member from the meeting should be recorded in the minutes of the meeting.

It is possible that your legislation and chosen book on rules of order do not explicitly require a Board member to leave a meeting because of a COI. It is still highly recommended that Board members with a COI leave the meeting even if they are not required to do so. They should do this in the organization's best interests.

If there is disagreement on whether a Board member is in conflict, the Board should discuss the matter and resolve it with the affected Board member in a closed meeting. Board members should not be offended by a suggestion that they may have a COI; instead, they should view it as an effort to uphold the integrity of the decision-making process.

It should be noted that holding a strong opinion on an issue is not in itself a conflict of interest. In addition, Board members should not declare conflict when many other people are similarly affected by the same decision or when the conflict is so remote that it is unlikely to impair their ability to act as impartial decision makers. When in doubt, the Board should consult a lawyer about whether a conflict exists.

# CHAPTER FOUR

# PROCEDURAL ISSUES

Procedural issues can create major problems for Boards and their effectiveness in a variety of ways. They can create dangerous situations in which the Board is indecisive, too hasty, or just poorly prepared. This chapter offers several solutions for such problems.

### PROBLEM

## 18

### BINDING DECISIONS AT GENERAL MEETINGS

The bylaws of a local organization stipulate that all motions passed by the members at an annual meeting do not require prior notice and are binding on the Board. In the heat of the moment during an annual meeting, a member moves that the CEO be fired, and the motion is passed.

#### Potential Damage

Decisions made on the spur of the moment, based on emotion or anger and without the benefit of professional input (in this case,

29

legal advice), can place the organization at risk. The CEO in this case may sue the organization for wrongful dismissal and defamation of character.

## Intervention

Some books on rules of order give the members present at annual meetings unlimited powers to adopt binding motions that the Board must implement. Such grassroots democracy becomes problematic when members do not have the knowledge to make informed and workable decisions or when discussions are driven by hype, emotion, and narrow interests. To prevent this, the bylaws should specify the areas in which an annual meeting can make binding decisions, with all other decisions deemed advisory to the Board.

In the short term, discourage impromptu motions at annual meetings of members or shareholders and explain why such decisions can be problematic. Suggest that members frame their motions as advisory, for example: *"Resolved, That the Board be requested to look into the possibility of {fill in the blank}."*

Over the long term, introduce a bylaw amendment that will redefine and clarify decision-making powers. For example: *"Except where these bylaws stipulate otherwise, votes taken at a general meeting shall be advisory in nature. The Board shall consider legal, operational, financial, and administrative issues, and may thereafter heed, modify, or refuse to abide by any advisory motions that were adopted, provided that the Board shall inform the members of its actions (or lack thereof) and the reasons for them."*

PROBLEM
# 19
## INSISTENCE ON UNANIMITY

Members of a Board insist on making all decisions by consensus and on having unanimous support for all motions. They don't want to annoy or upset any of the members and are afraid of the dire consequences if a decision is adopted with some dissenting votes.

## Potential Damage

Although it is usually desirable to listen to all views and accommodate all legitimate interests, there may come a time when a decision needs to be made despite dissent. Insistence on unanimity can unjustly dilute, stall, or block a good decision, as petulant individuals promoting narrow interests refuse to budge. Insistence on unanimity in such cases can give veto power to one individual, with the Board becoming paralyzed by this tyranny of the minority.

Insistence on unanimity can also have the effect of indirectly stifling dissent. It can make it awkward for individuals to take an honest and principled position and vote against a motion, for fear that their negative votes will cause discomfort among their colleagues.

## Intervention

Help the Board develop comfort with differences of opinion and learn to tolerate—or even benefit from—controversies. Emphasize that although it is generally preferable to listen to all views and, if possible, arrive at unanimous decisions, there are times when the Board will be duty-bound to move forward with only a majority vote. Dissenting votes should not be seen as a bad thing as long as all legitimate views have been heard, understood, and considered.

## PROBLEM
## 20
## RUSHED DECISIONS

A Board finds itself close to the end of a meeting with only half the agenda completed. No one wants to leave any unfinished business nor is anyone prepared to extend the time of the meeting. The Board thus rushes the process and makes its remaining decisions in a hurry.

### Potential Damage

In its haste, the Board may fail to pay attention to important details. Members who have questions and concerns may be afraid to present them since they do not want to slow things down or anger their rushed colleagues. The potential for flawed decisions is very high.

### Intervention

If possible, extend the duration of the meeting. If not, prioritize the remaining items and deal only with high priority issues at this meeting. Postpone other items to the next meeting.

Next time, plan a realistic agenda, with tentative time limits allocated to the main issues. Start the meeting on time and monitor the clock throughout the meeting. Advise members regularly on how much time is left for an issue and how many agenda items remain to be dealt with. Being so advised, members will hopefully avoid rambling, digressions, and other time-wasting habits.

# 21
## LAST-MINUTE AGENDA ITEMS ("GREEN BANANAS")

At the start of a meeting, a Chair asks if members have anything to add to the agenda. Several items are added without background material, and some of them are substantial or controversial. Presenters expect the Board to make decisions on these last-minute items.

### Potential Damage

Pressing ahead with items that are not ripe for decision making (so-called "green bananas") is risky for a number of reasons. First, Board members may be surprised, uncomfortable, and resentful, and this may distract them from the business at hand. Second, low-grade discussions and flawed decisions may result from the lack of prior analysis and pre-reading of background material. Third, those who missed the meeting may feel ambushed and may resent being left out of the process since the items were not included on the agenda that was circulated prior to the meeting.

In the case of a public body, citizens who missed the meeting may go as far as challenging the validity of some decisions, claiming that—had they known about certain last-minute items—they would have made a special effort to attend and possibly speak to the Board at the meeting.

### Intervention

There may be no harm if the last-minute items are only discussed, but forcing a decision on them may be a costly mistake. Unless the decision must be made urgently, it is probably safer and healthier to let the green banana ripen by postponing it to a subsequent meeting.

As a preventive measure, teach your Board to operate less reactively and more proactively, with most agenda items planned and with last-minute items being the exception and not the norm. Board members who want to add agenda items should contact the Chair at least a few days before a meeting so items can be prioritized in the context of the other agenda items. It should be understood that late additions may need to be postponed to a subsequent meeting.

It may also be prudent to institute a green banana policy, whereby adding last-minute items to the agenda requires the Board's agreement (by at least a majority vote). Such a policy will establish a professional and measured approach to decision making. In the case of a public body, it will assure the community that it will be informed in advance of decisions (except possibly for emergencies). Such a policy will thereby entrench greater transparency and accountability.

PROBLEM

## 22

## POOR PREPARATION

Some Board members open premeeting packages five minutes before the meeting begins. On some Boards, it is the Chair who behaves in this way. In other settings, most background material is not precirculated but is handed out at the start of a meeting. In both situations, Board members are poorly prepared.

### Potential Damage

Unprepared Board members slow meetings down with questions that are often covered in premeeting packages. Alternatively, they may keep quiet, rely on experienced members, or trust the CEO's judgment without questioning. Their capacity to make informed decisions is small, and the likelihood of flawed decisions increases. Members who did their preparation may become resentful and cynical, which may distract them at the meeting. If the culprit is the Chair, his or her action (or inaction) validates the notion that lack of preparation is okay, thereby perpetuating the problem.

## Intervention

If a specific issue on the agenda is significant, pause to give people time to review the relevant material or to have its key points explained. If a decision on the issue can wait, it may be prudent to postpone it until the next meeting and remind members to prepare for it.

As a preventive measure, emphasize during orientation that a Board is not a social club and that members have a duty to act diligently and responsibly and prepare for meetings so they can make informed decisions. Emphasize that members must never assume that report writers have done a thorough job and are incapable of making mistakes.

As an additional measure, insist that most materials be ready for review a few days before the meeting and that late reports be the rare exception rather than the norm. Finally, ask report writers to make their documents clear, concise, and easy to read. Lengthy reports should include tables of contents and executive summaries, to make it easy for members to locate key points. It is also a good practice to prewrite potential decision-making options or motions and to highlight them in premeeting materials.

PROBLEM

# 23

# DISORGANIZED PROBLEM SOLVING

The problem-solving process on a particular Board is disorganized. In one case, the discussion is started by a Board member who strongly advocates a solution without clearly identifying the problem. In another case, a variety of solutions are suggested, and the Board—in its haste to move on—latches on to the most obvious solution and makes its decision. It feels like shooting before aiming.

## Potential Damage

Without an organized problem-solving process, the quality of decisions often suffers, especially when issues are complex or controversial. The fact that a solution feels like it might work is not enough. A deliberate problem-solving process is needed, or else costly flaws may be discovered during the implementation stages. Without an organized problem-solving process, people will rightly ask: *"What exact problem are we attempting to solve?"*

## Intervention

A problem-solving process should not start with a focus on solutions. Instead, there should be a sophisticated, organized, logical progression and thoughtful analysis, especially if an issue is complex or controversial. There may be as many as six stages to problem solving:

1. Clearly defining the problems that need to be solved

2. Identifying the criteria for an optimal solution (fair, legal, affordable, enforceable, etc.)

3. Brainstorming for potential solutions

4. Evaluating potential solutions against the agreed-upon criteria (see step 2)

5. Choosing the best solution, which may combine elements of several options

6. Establishing an implementation plan for the chosen solution

In order to ensure a disciplined and organized problem-solving process, it may be beneficial to retain an impartial facilitator, especially when the stakes are high.

A member who believes the Board has moved too quickly to "solution-mode" should not hesitate to say: *"I am having some trouble here. Before we talk about solutions and make any decisions, can someone help me identify what exact problem we are trying to solve?"*

PROBLEM

## 24

# IMPROMPTU MOTIONS

A Board member stumbles as he attempts to articulate a motion, and the result is a poorly worded and flawed motion. Another member promptly seconds the motion and the Board debates and adopts it, despite the fact that the motion is confusing and ambiguous. Everyone is expecting the CEO or the minute taker to clean up the wording later.

## Potential Damage

Risk levels rise as the Board makes vaguely worded decisions that commit organizational resources and the future of the community. Working in this manner can be seen as amateurish and irresponsible and would likely not command the trust and respect of the community. This practice is equivalent to signing a contract with the key words left blank.

Expecting the CEO or the minute taker to interpret the wishes of the Board is unfair and unreasonable to both the staff and the community. At a subsequent meeting, Board members may get angry with the CEO or staff if they interpreted their wishes incorrectly—even though those wishes were not articulated clearly in the first place.

### Intervention

Regardless of whether you are the Chair or a Board member, insist that motions be concise, unambiguous, and complete and that they be written down before any vote on them is taken. The preferred practice is to have motions prewritten and included in staff or committee reports to ensure that they are the product of careful consideration. This will also provide all Board members with the opportunity to review and consider such motions before the meeting.

If no Board member raises concerns about a poorly worded impromptu motion, the CEO or the minute taker should not hesitate to intervene: "Can you please put the motion in writing?" or "Can I read the motion and confirm that I captured it correctly?"

PROBLEM

# 25

## PREMATURE CLOSURE

A Board member gets impatient with the debate and yells out: *"I call the question,"* meaning that he wants to close the debate and vote on the motion. Despite the fact that some members still want to speak, the Chair claims that her hands are tied and she closes the debate. The Board then takes a vote on the motion that was the subject of the debate.

## Potential Damage

Members waiting to speak are left behind, along with any good ideas or insights they might have offered. Without the input that was cut off, the quality of the decision may be reduced. The members who were cut off may feel disenfranchised. The level of support for the decision may therefore diminish, and people may even work to block implementation of the decision, not necessarily because of the decision itself but because they were stifled at the demand of one person.

## Intervention

In nonadversarial settings, there should be no need for motions to close debate. Discussions should end naturally when people have nothing new to add and are ready to vote. To reduce repetition and conserve time, members can be urged at the start of a meeting to make their comments focused and concise, and they may be given extra reminders when needed.

In contrast, motions to close debate may be necessary in adversarial settings, in which some individuals want to close the debate and others are deliberately stalling it. However, the decision to close debate is not made by one member calling the question, nor is it made unilaterally by the Chair. Rather, the decision to close debate is made by the Board collectively. Under several books on rules of order, the decision to close debate requires a two-thirds vote.

## QUICK VOTES

During the meeting of one organization, debate ends and the Chair speeds through the vote: *"In favor—opposed—carried."* In another organization, the Chair seizes the moment when vague consensus emerges and says: *"Are we all in agreement to do this? If so, let's move on. Time is running short."*

### Potential Damage

With a quick vote, it is very likely that members will not know what they are voting on, and this is not fair to them or to the organization and the community that they serve. Subsequent arguments about what exactly was voted on are sure to occur, which is bound to increase anxiety and erode trust and confidence in the decision-making process.

### Intervention

Slow down and treat the moment of voting as a sacred moment. Confirm that the Board is ready to vote and knows the precise wording of the motion, and only then take the vote.

## OBSESSION WITH RULES

A Board is accustomed to doing everything by the rule book. It insists on motions and formal votes, even on unimportant decisions such as taking a break. Amendments are processed using a highly structured approach. Procedure is deemed very important, and the Board often enlists the help of an expert on parliamentary procedure.

As a variation on this problem, some Boards become obsessed with a definition of the governance model or book under which they operate: Is it the Carver model of Policy Governance? Is it *Robert's Rules of Order*? Is the Board in compliance with the chosen model at any given time?

## Potential Damage

In its quest to do things exactly right (a focus on procedure), the Board may lose its focus on doing the right things (a focus on substance). An overuse of formal procedures tends to stifle and constrain debate and prevent natural flow and creative thinking. Excessive formality and rigidity are bound to limit the depth of discussions and the quality of decisions. Enlightened individuals may be turned off by the excessive formality and refuse to join the Board.

## Intervention

Explain to your Board that its primary focus should be substantive (making quality decisions). The essential intent of rules of order is to balance the need for democracy, inclusiveness, and fairness with the need for effective time management. Most Boards work collaboratively and do not require hundreds of pages of rules on how to be fair, inclusive, and efficient. Fees for parliamentary experts may be high and are justified only if they provide substantial value.

Arguments about Carver versus *Robert's Rules* are often confusing, misguided, and wasteful. The Carver model addresses Board governance, while *Robert's Rules of Order* address only meeting procedures. Comparing the two is like comparing apples and oranges. Bring the arguments about Carver versus *Robert's Rules* to an end, unless you have the appropriate expert in the room. Just focus your Board on making quality decisions, together, and at a comfortable pace. If you do this, the model you use will likely be less significant.

PROBLEM
28

## PROCEDURAL TRICKERY

A Municipal Council member uses his knowledge of rules of order (parliamentary procedure) to advance proposals of questionable merit or to stall or block other initiatives. In another setting, the Board of a charity looks for a way to circumvent its bylaws in order to forego a requirement to notify its members or the community of an upcoming contentious decision.

### Potential Damage

Using rules of order strategically to boost certain causes or block others means that the merits of a proposal become less important than the proponent's knowledge of the rules. A low-grade proposal may be adopted not on its merits but because its proponent is procedurally savvy. Conversely, a high-quality proposal may be lost because its proponent does not know the rules. Clearly, these dynamics are highly flawed and undermine the goal of making quality decisions. They are not fair to individuals and are ultimately damaging to the organization.

Using a technical loophole to circumvent a fundamental requirement such as notice to the membership or the community is dishonest and manipulative and amounts to procedural trickery. The members will eventually expose this maneuver. The credibility of the Board will then be diminished, and restoring it will require a great deal of work.

### Intervention

Teach your Board that process should never overtake substance and suggest that members not use rules of order as weapons or manipulative tools. Have a frank conversation with members who attempt to get their way through procedural trickery. Explain that rules are intended to facilitate progress and engage members in shared decision making, as equal partners, and that their purpose is not to confuse, intimidate, manipulate, or bully others.

Avoid and refuse to tolerate the use of technical loopholes, especially when they compromise fundamental principles and offend the integrity of the decision-making process.

PROBLEM

# 29

## MINUTES THAT FOCUS ON INDIVIDUAL WORDS AND ACTIONS

At the insistence of the Chair or vocal Board members, minutes of Board meetings become a detailed verbatim record of what people said. The minutes also show the names of movers and seconders of motions and record how every member voted on every issue.

### Potential Damage

Board members may not read lengthy verbatim minutes and may therefore forget to perform their follow-up duties. In addition, verbatim minutes are sometimes embarrassing and often lead to arguments: *"I did not say this, and—even if I did—I didn't mean to."* People may be afraid to speak in meetings, knowing that each word will be recorded, and this may hamper creativity and spontaneity.

Recording names of movers and seconders in minutes creates

the impression that the mover and seconder supported a motion, when ultimately this may not have been the case. In addition, recording these names conveys the false impression that the individuals own the respective motion, when in fact they do not.

Recording how individuals voted diverts attention from the actions of the Board as a collective decision-making body and focuses on individual actions. This may convey the false impression that the accountability for decisions is personal, when in fact it is collective.

## Intervention

First, abandon the practice of verbatim minutes. The two alternatives to verbatim minutes are *decisions-only minutes* (capturing decisions and follow-up items) and *anecdotal minutes* (adding concise point form summaries of discussions, without attributing comments to individuals). Anecdotal summaries should be omitted for closed meetings, which deal with sensitive and confidential matters.

Second, establish a policy that names of movers and seconders are not recorded in minutes.

Finally, establish a policy on recorded votes. It seems appropriate to record votes in public bodies, since elected members may want to campaign on their voting records. Even then, the practice should be limited to recording only dissenting votes and only on request. Conversely, with a nongovernmental Board, collective actions are more significant than individual votes, and there should usually be no need to record individual votes. One potential reason for recording a person's vote is if the individual genuinely believes the Board acted recklessly, fraudulently, or illegally. In such a case, the member may find it advisable to resign from the Board.

CHAPTER FIVE

# PROBLEMATIC BOARD MEMBERS

As an equal partner on the Board, each member must understand the decision-making process, respect it, and be prepared to defend it when needed. This chapter describes problems that diminish the ability of Board members to function in this manner. The root causes of dysfunctional behaviors by Board members include weak selection and orientation processes, unclear roles and responsibilities, and a lack of feedback (see Appendix B for Board evaluation tools).

## PROBLEM
# 30
## THE DISENGAGED BOARD MEMBER

The disengaged Board member does not prepare for meetings, arrives late, reviews e-mails during meetings, leaves early, or misses meetings altogether. He usually does not take on any follow-up duties, and—when he does—he is a master of excuses for not getting things done. On some Boards, it is the Chair who acts in this way, thereby validating such behaviors.

### Potential Damage

With low commitment levels from a disengaged member (or members), the Board operates at less than full capacity. Without the disengaged member's wisdom and active participation, the quality of Board decisions may suffer. Other Board members may need to carry more of the workload to compensate for his inactivity, which may lead to resentment, mistrust, and burnout. The increased dependency on active Board members is likely to create a leadership gap and weaken the Board when the active members leave.

### Intervention

Find out if this individual is genuinely interested in the Board's work, and—if so—demand a higher commitment level from him or assign him specific tasks along with reporting deadlines. On the other hand, if Board work is not a priority for him, you may need to request that he step aside and make room for other individuals who want to serve on the Board with full commitment.

To prevent this problem, enhance your recruitment and orientation processes. Make sure that prospective Board members have the right combination of knowledge, skills, and attitude. Make sure they know the required time commitment and are prepared to give it. Avoid using recruitment solely to reward people who have been around for a long time. Avoid enticing people by telling them that Board service is a good thing to have on a resume. Discourage those who want to serve on the Board mainly for visibility and influence or to gain contacts and thereby promote their careers or businesses.

## PROBLEM
# 31
# THE SINGLE-ISSUE ADVOCATE

The single-issue advocate cares only about a specific topic or matter. For example, a member of a Municipal Council campaigned on a promise to block new construction projects. She is fully involved when such projects are debated, but she pays little or no attention to other issues. She often trades her vote with those of other members in exchange for support of her motions.

## Potential Damage

The community receives less than the full scope of leadership that it is entitled to. Cynicism develops toward the council, and its credibility diminishes. Moreover, when members trade their votes with specific outcomes in mind, they come to meetings with closed minds and are incapable of learning from debates and making informed and balanced decisions.

## Intervention

Speak to this member privately and clarify that her role is to work for the community as a whole and on all issues, and that campaign promises must not be allowed to negatively affect her work on the council. Refuse to trade votes with her.

To prevent this problem, clarify during Board orientation that members must place the interests of the community ahead of other interests. Emphasize that they must attend to all issues that come up for decision making and attend meetings with open minds.

# PROBLEM
# 32
## THE REBEL

This Board member rebels against any real or perceived authority. He portrays himself as the conscience of the community and a champion of transparency and accountability. He therefore on some occasions reveals details that were discussed in closed meetings. On other occasions, he speaks to the media and chastises the Board for having made certain decisions. He enjoys the public attention he receives and appears to thrive on his ability to annoy his colleagues. Some Board members refer to him as a one-person destruction machine.

## Potential Damage

If a Board is truly dysfunctional, a rebel may indeed help bring it back on track. However, in many instances, rebel behaviors poison the air. In addition, rebel members may not be listened to or taken seriously by their annoyed colleagues, even if their points are significant. This is bound to diminish the quality of Board decisions and to increase organizational risk.

The Board's standing may also suffer. Leaks from closed meetings and postmeeting attacks on duly made Board decisions tend to diminish trust and reduce the Board's credibility in the community.

## Intervention

Speak to the rebel privately and give him constructive feedback. Share the observation that his input and insights are often astute and significant, but the fact that he works outside the system and undermines other Board members may be preventing his wisdom from helping the community that he cares about. Suggest that he communicate in a respectful and supportive manner, which would make it easier for others to listen to him and learn from his wisdom. Remind him of his duty to keep confidentiality and avoid undermining duly made Board decisions.

If no improvement is evident despite your genuine and concerted efforts to achieve cooperation, you may need to act in the interests of the community that your Board serves and examine punitive measures, which may include censure or even removal from the Board.

Ultimately, you need to address the root causes of this problem. Reinforce your Board member selection processes to attract effective individuals and prevent misguided people from joining it. Ensure that all members understand their roles and responsibilities. Communicate regularly with your community and listen and respond fully to its needs. This way, your Board will be trusted and respected, and rebels without a constructive cause will not be rewarded by the community's attention and support.

PROBLEM

# 33

# THE ACCUSER

This Board member reacts to decisions she does not like with dramatic allegations of conspiracies and hidden agendas. She accuses leaders of maliciously violating individual rights. She often does this based on limited data and without checking all the facts.

She stubbornly refuses to back off and will not consider reasonable explanations that cast doubt on her allegations.

## Potential Damage

Members may hesitate to take on leadership roles for fear that every action they take would come under the microscope and that any innocent mistakes would be interpreted as malicious acts. Leaders may decline to make necessary but unpopular decisions for fear that they will be accused of hidden agendas. Those who chair meetings may treat the accuser leniently and allow her to dominate for fear that enforcing the rules would be seen as a conspiracy. Indeed, conspiracy theories may become self-fulfilling prophecies, as frustrated members begin to work together to find ways to cope with the accuser. The climate is likely to become toxic, thereby distracting the Board and reducing its ability to make quality decisions.

## Intervention

Speak to the accuser privately. Find out why she acts the way she does, and see what can be done to address any legitimate concerns she has. Explain the damage that her negative tone inflicts on the Board's ability to serve the community, and ask her to help make it safe for people to speak without fear of being accused of hidden motives. Encourage her to learn all the facts before leveling an accusation. Indicate your intention to act as fairly as possible toward her and others, and state that no one—including her—will be permitted to dominate. Indicate that, as a human being, you will make the odd mistake, and ask not to be judged harshly for it.

As additional measures, strengthen your meeting procedures and make them fair and above board, so there is less for any accuser to complain about. Invite Board members to give you feedback and let you know if you overlook something while running a meeting.

## THE BULLY

This vocal member thinks that by talking loudly and belligerently, he can intimidate others to act the way he wants. Say he misses a meeting during which a contentious decision was made. At the next meeting, he asks indignantly why he was not consulted. He threatens to take certain actions unless the decision is reversed. In order to restore calm, the Board backs down and cancels its earlier decision.

### Potential Damage

Members may be intimidated and silenced into acquiescing to the bully. Good decisions may be aborted, and flawed decisions may be pushed through. Some members may get frustrated by the bullying, while others may see it as a model for them to follow. Meaningful democracy—where all Board members are treated as equal partners and where decisions are based on merit—is inadvertently replaced by bullying, otherwise called the "tyranny of the minority."

### Intervention

Speak up: *"Rick, if you have concerns about a decision, we'll hear them, but we need you to express them in a manner that shows respect for the Board."* If the bullying member's concerns are valid, the decision may need to be revisited. If not, the Board should have the backbone to carry on with it. In any event, the threatening tone should not be tolerated. The Board must act on the merits of the input without being distracted by the loudness of the argument.

## PROBLEM
## 35
# THE KNOW-IT-ALL

A Board member acts like a know-it-all. She speaks in an arrogant, condescending, and conceited manner, as though meetings are her platform to showcase her fancy terminology and bring the voice of experience to the uninitiated.

## Potential Damage

Members may react negatively or stop listening when the know-it-all speaks, even when she presents useful and relevant information. The member's arrogant style and demeanor may become a barrier to her valuable input and her ability to contribute to the decision-making process.

## Intervention

If you notice members tuning out when the know-it-all speaks, ask the group to pay attention. After the meeting, give the know-it-all feedback. Let her know how she comes across. Suggest that she make it easier for colleagues to listen to her by adding a dose of humility and graciousness to her comments.

## PROBLEM
## 36
# THE CONTRARIAN

This Board member instantly finds flaws in every new idea. His favorite two words are *"yes, but."* He listens intently to views with which he agrees but otherwise stops paying attention or gets busy formulating a rebuttal. He routinely interrupts others in midsentence.

## Potential Damage

As a result of the contrarian member's actions, creativity and innovation are stifled and the Board's ability to fully explore new ideas is compromised. The predictable obstacles frustrate members who initiate new ideas to solve complex problems. These members may eventually stop trying or quit the Board altogether. The Board stands to lose effective members together with their talents and good ideas.

## Intervention

Do not allow the contrarian to interrupt. Consider a private talk with him to share observations about his behavior and its impact on the Board's deliberations. Challenge him to propose solutions instead of always opposing them.

Speak to the Board about how to respond when they are interrupted before being fully heard: *"I need to finish"* or *"May I finish, please?"* Encourage people to listen with the intent of learning and to resist the temptation to quickly simplify, generalize, assume, or draw conclusions, especially when the issues are complex. Emphasize that *"yes, but"* is a verbal eraser, with the emphatic *but* erasing the *yes*.

As a nonconventional intervention, you could establish this procedure with the group: If a member interrupts, he or she may be asked to summarize what the other individual said or meant to say, with a symbolic fine imposed if the summary is inaccurate.

PROBLEM

# 37

# THE CLOSET PARLIAMENTARIAN

This Board member persistently raises points of order on obscure and seemingly irrelevant points of parliamentary procedure, such as the "correct" way to amend a motion, in what cases a motion must be seconded, and so on.

## Potential Damage

Progress slows down and time is wasted on procedural issues, possibly distracting the Board from the substantive decisions being discussed. Members may get intimidated and confused, but they fear that they have no option but to heed the closet parliamentarian's points. She may end up dictating the actual decisions, and collective Board control may therefore be lost.

## Intervention

Educate all members that rules of order are intended to facilitate progress rather than impede it, and that they are a means to an end and not an end in itself. Emphasize that rules should be applied in a manner that includes members in decision making on an equal basis, rather than to confuse, intimidate, or frustrate them. You may quote *Robert's Rules of Order,* Newly Revised (Perseus Publishing, 10th edition), which suggests that *"In ordinary meetings it is undesirable to raise points of order on minor irregularities of a purely technical character, if it is clear that no one's rights are being infringed upon and no real harm is being done to the proper transaction of business."* (For sample myths and truths on rules of order, see Appendix C.)

PROBLEM

# 38

# THE SHORT-TEMPERED BOARD MEMBER

The short-tempered Board member loses his temper and becomes loud, abusive, and threatening, especially when things don't go his way. He insults his colleagues and openly questions their competence, motivation, or integrity. When he believes his views were distorted or his track record was misrepresented, he goes on the attack and insists on setting the record straight.

## Potential Damage

The environment becomes toxic. Members find it unsafe to share their ideas and may constantly worry that they might trigger a temperamental reaction from this member. Indeed, his emotional outbursts are sometimes deliberate tactics to intimidate, bully, and stifle others and thereby achieve certain outcomes or prevent others. The Board's ability to act as a mature and professional decision-making body is diminished. Flawed decisions are very likely.

## Intervention

One option is to call a break and give the temperamental member feedback privately. If this does not work, you may need to address his behavior in front of others. Ask the individual to lower the volume and soften the tone of his comments. Stress that he must focus on issues and not people, and ask him to help make it safe for others to speak. Refuse to capitulate to emotional outbursts and do not accept compromises and low-grade solutions, just for the sake of appeasing this temperamental member and achieving peace and harmony.

As a preventive measure, if you anticipate such behaviors, open the meeting by noting that the issues may be tough, but then ask members to help you create a safe environment and to act in a manner that will command trust and respect from the community that they care about.

PROBLEM

# 39

## THE OVERLY SENSITIVE BOARD MEMBER

This Board member takes things very personally. For example, say she is the author of a report and gets very hurt when Board members question its findings or conclusions. When the Board decides to take a different route than the report recommends, she becomes visibly upset or even bursts into tears, taking things much too personally. Those who asked questions apologize profusely and promise not to offend or upset her again.

### Potential Damage

If the member is so sensitive and attached to the report, it is awkward to ask questions and give the topic the necessary scrutiny. Indeed, a weak Board may be persuaded to make a flawed decision or abort or dilute a good one in an effort to avoid hurting the feelings of such a member. Under such conditions, honest and full debate becomes a rare occurrence.

### Intervention

Acknowledge the work done by the member and express appreciation for it, and then stress the importance of making it easy for others to ask questions. Emphasize that questions and feedback are not personal attacks but a crucial component of effective decision making. Conversely, remind Board members to keep the tone of their questions and concerns constructive and to focus on the content of the report and not the abilities of its author.

In some instances, it may be best to call a break and find out what triggered the member's emotional reaction. If the reason was a hurtful personal comment that had gone unnoticed, remind the Board to be sensitive and respectful of others. If the individual's points were misunderstood and unjustifiably dismissed, bring those issues to the Board's attention after the break. On the other hand, if the individual is just too sensitive, emphasize the need for her to develop a thick skin, to not take things personally, and to not allow her emotional reaction to block valid concerns.

As an additional measure, whenever possible, delegate work on contentious issues to individuals who are competent, mature, confident, and open to feedback. Ideally, authors of reports will have anticipated significant concerns and addressed them proactively within their reports.

PROBLEM

# 40

## THE SECRETIVE BOARD MEMBER

This member withholds crucial information that was given to her privately by staff or community members, since she has promised them secrecy.

### Potential Damage

Withholding relevant information (gained privately under a promise to keep it secret) is very problematic and can place the organization at risk. For example, if a staff member complains secretly to a Board member about workplace harassment and the Board is not made aware of the complaint, it cannot address this serious issue in a decisive and timely manner.

### Intervention

Establish with the Board that no promises of secrecy should be given to outside parties when the information they share is critical to Board decision making or points to organizational risk.

PROBLEM

# 41

## THE TALKATIVE BOARD MEMBER

A knowledgeable or passionate Board member may dominate the discussion and take up most of the time, making the meeting appear like a dialogue between him and other talkative members. Quieter members (the thinkers), together with their knowledge and insights, are left behind.

### Potential Damage

The scope of discussions is limited and decisions may be narrowly based and of low quality. The sense of partnership is diminished, as most members are left in the position of passive spectators. Later, if a decision proves to be flawed, quieter members may blame dominant ones for it. In fact, quieter members share the blame, since it is their duty to speak up and act as full partners in the process, despite the imperfectly run meeting or their dominating, talkative colleagues.

### Intervention

Thank the talkers for their input and then invite the thinkers to share their ideas: *"Thank you, Jane and Patrick. We need to hear from people who have not spoken. How about you, Ted? You have expertise in financial planning. Do you have any observations for us?"* Or try this: *"This issue seems a bit complex, and it may be productive to give each person a chance to make a brief comment. Does this sound reasonable? Okay, but brief comments only, please, and if you have nothing to add, just say 'pass.' Starting with you, Becky . . ."*

Yet another method of engaging quieter members in discussion and neutralizing the effect of dominating members is to set aside a few minutes of silence, during which members jot down their thoughts on a specific question. After the period of silence, invite individuals to share their thoughts, starting with the quietest ones.

PROBLEM
## 42
## THE BOARD MEMBER WHO WON'T SPEAK UP

The Board member who won't speak up prefers to stay safe and quiet. She may see problems with decisions and the way meetings are run, but she says nothing, perhaps because she is new to the Board. She tells the Board Chair that she'll offer her views only if asked to do so. She may vote against motions for reasons that no one knows.

A variation of this problem occurs when management and staff members hesitate to share important information for fear of repercussions or attacks by vocal Board members.

### Potential Damage

Without this member's wisdom and expertise, problems may go unnoticed and the quality of decisions may suffer. Even if the current Chair knows this member's style and makes an effort to engage her in discussions, it is unfair to expect future Chairs to compensate for her lack of proactivity and to know when she should be prompted to speak.

## Intervention

During Board orientation, emphasize that all members are equal and full partners in decision making and that there is no probation or trial period for new members. Inform them that newness is not an excuse for silence or inaction. Clarify that asking questions or raising concerns is not only acceptable but an integral part of their roles, and failure to do so amounts to dereliction of duty. In addition, establish that management and staff members are also expected to share significant information, and reassure them that there will be no repercussions for sharing information that might be uncomfortable for some Board members to hear.

Tell members the story of a Board member—an accountant—who remained silent when a highly popular but flawed investment decision was made, for fear of upsetting others. When the investment became problematic, it was discovered that the member in question knew of the flaws but had kept quiet. His colleagues then initiated court action against him, on the premise that it was his duty to speak up against the proposal despite the exuberant enthusiasm for it.

PROBLEM

# 43

## THE MUMBLER

This knowledgeable, perceptive, and astute Board member mumbles or speaks in another way that makes it difficult for others to understand him, for example, speaking very fast or with a heavy accent.

## Potential Damage

The Board may miss important information, and its capacity to benefit from this member's insights and ideas is diminished. The quality of the Board's decisions may suffer.

### Intervention

The Chair or any member should ask this member to raise his voice, speak more slowly, enunciate his words, or—if appropriate—put his key points down in writing. Let him know that the group values his knowledge but has a hard time understanding him. Further options to improve the situation include communications courses or private coaching to help make this member more articulate.

P R O B L E M

# 44

## THE LECTURER

A Board member speaks to the Board for an extended period on a highly technical topic, and there appears to be no end in sight. During the question period that follows, each of the presenter's answers becomes a lecture in itself. (This problem can also involve professional advisers or staff members who make presentations to the Board.)

### Potential Damage

Unless the speaker is exceptionally engaging, members become saturated and bored. By the time the meeting resumes after the speaker finishes, the freshness and momentum of the group are lost, and it is difficult to regain them. The group's ability to listen and address subsequent agenda items with fresh minds is reduced. In addition, less time is available for the remaining items, and they may end up being rushed, thereby increasing the risk of flawed decisions.

### Intervention

You may just have to interrupt the speaker and ask how much more time he or she needs. Alternatively, indicate that time is running short, and suggest five minutes to wrap up the talk.

As a preventive measure, negotiate a time frame with speakers prior to meetings, establish how you will let them know when their time is running out, and encourage them to keep their answers to questions concise, in order to accommodate as many questions as possible.

**CHAPTER SIX**

# THE INEFFECTIVE BOARD CHAIR

As the organization's chief elected officer, the Chair has the role of providing leadership to the Board and presiding over its meetings. As a voting member of the Board, the Chair has the same voting rights as other members. The Chair does not have the power to make unilateral decisions, except where the organization's bylaws or policies provide otherwise. This chapter discusses problems at the Board Chair's level. See Appendix B for a Board Chair evaluation form, and Appendix D for tools for meeting Chairs.

In order to perform his or her duties effectively, the Chair should know what they are. Typically, the Chair's roles between meetings are to:

- Serve as the Board's official spokesperson, representing its policies and decisions.

- Assist Board members, offer guidance, and share knowledge and expertise with them.

■ Provide guidance to the CEO, in compliance with Board policies and decisions.

■ Facilitate emergency decisions and bring them to the Board for ratification at a later point.

■ Prepare meeting agendas, with input from management and Board members.

■ Follow up between meetings to ensure that delegated tasks are completed.

■ Mediate disputes among Board members.

The Chair's roles during meetings are to:

■ Start the meeting on time and keep it on track and on time.

■ Set the tone, direction, and speaking guidelines for the meeting.

■ Ensure that the agenda and the various items on it are clearly explained.

■ Facilitate structured debates without stifling creativity.

■ Maintain a dynamic yet comfortable pace for the meeting.

■ Pay attention to verbal and nonverbal signals and respond to them in a timely manner.

■ Monitor the mood of the meeting and change directions when needed.

■ Ensure that the background for an agenda item is clear before discussion begins.

■ Raise questions and stimulate in-depth discussions among Board members.

■ Provide periodic summaries and lead to closure and decision making.

■ Ensure that decisions and motions are clearly articulated before taking any votes.

■ Ensure that the minute taker has the necessary details to record accurate summaries.

■ Engage quieter members (and their knowledge and ideas), and prevent domination by more forceful members.

■ Detect Boardroom problems and intervene in a timely, firm, and respectful manner.

■ Publicly recognize members for their contributions and celebrate their achievements.

■ Add a light touch and appropriate humor as appropriate.

■ Vary the pace of the meeting and make it interesting and engaging.

PROBLEM
## 45
## THE CHAIR WHO BIASES DISCUSSIONS

During meetings, this Board Chair refuses—or conveniently forgets—to recognize members with whom he disagrees or whom he does not like. When pressed to facilitate a democratic debate and voting, the Chair refuses and maintains tight control over the meeting. When it appears as though a key vote may not go his way, he threatens to resign.

### Potential Damage

Discussions lack depth and are narrowly focused. The ability to explore new perspectives is minimal, and the Board's ability to make creative and informed decisions is hampered. In addition, members may resent being ignored. They may therefore become disengaged or, alternatively, plot strategies to undermine the Chair. Noncombatants may find it unsafe to speak in this toxic environment, thereby depriving the Board of their observations. In some cases, support for a positive initiative may diminish because of the Chair's behavior.

## Intervention

Remind the Chair that all Board members must be treated as equal partners in the decision-making process and that he must make room for different views to emerge, regardless of what they are and whether he approves or disapproves of the presenters. If needed, call for a break and give your feedback to the Chair in private.

As a preventive measure, during Board orientation, clarify the Chair's role as a facilitator of shared decision making. Teach Board members that *suffering is optional* and that they should not hesitate to question counterproductive behaviors by the Chair or others. Suggest that by allowing such behaviors to go unchallenged, members are in effect condoning them and thereby diminishing the Board's capacity to make quality decisions.

PROBLEM

46

## THE CHAIR WHO ACTS UNILATERALLY

This Board Chair has a significant and costly project in mind. She bypasses the Board and intimidates and bullies the CEO and staff into undertaking the project without Board approval.

## Potential Damage

When the Board is being bypassed and the staff is being bullied by the Chair's unilateral actions, collective scrutiny and risk analysis are minimal or nonexistent. The organization may be stuck with a costly and misguided undertaking for years to come. To add insult to injury, the Board may be held collectively responsible for the consequences of the Chair's unilateral actions. In addition, when the Board discovers that it was bypassed, members will be angry and trust levels will diminish.

## Intervention

There are many misconceptions about the role of the Chair. Some picture a Chair who knows how to give orders and overpower strong personalities. However, an effective Chair will not impose her will on the Board but will act as a mentor and facilitator of shared decision making. In fact, an effective Board Chair knows how to "dance" with the Board. She intuitively knows when to lead and when to follow, when to speak and when to listen, and when to be proactive instead of reactive. Dancing effectively fosters a true sense of partnership with the Board.

Confront the Chair and hold her accountable for acting unilaterally and thereby potentially placing the organization at risk. If needed, consider disciplinary measures against her. If the Chair's unilateral actions can be reversed, seek the Board's collective direction on this option.

As an additional measure, try to determine what systemic weaknesses may have caused the Chair to believe that it was okay or necessary to act unilaterally. Such weaknesses may include unclear or unexplained roles and responsibilities, poorly written policies on reporting and accountability, an indecisive or acquiescent Board, and a slow strategic progress.

To prevent such behaviors, present the scenario given in this problem as a case study during Board orientation, and emphasize that abuses of power will not be tolerated on your Board. Clarify to the CEO and staff that if any Board Chair bypasses the Board, they are duty-bound to say no and refer the matter to the full Board.

It should be noted that emergencies may make it necessary for the Chair to act unilaterally. In such cases (which should be the exception and not the norm), the Chair should report to the Board on any unilateral actions taken and seek the Board's ratification. Your Board should establish the extent of unilateral decision making that it is willing to tolerate and the circumstances that will justify it.

PROBLEM

# 47

# THE SPINELESS CHAIR

The spineless Chair likes to please people and hesitates to do anything that might offend anyone. He remains silent when vocal members dominate and others are left behind, together with their knowledge and ideas. He tolerates digressions, rambling, and nasty personal attacks on Board members and staff. When members make motions that are ill advised or out of order, he just states the motions and invites debate on them.

## Potential Damage

This Chair's overriding goal of pleasing people and avoiding hurt feelings and his reluctance to address unacceptable behaviors may damage the decision-making process. Unless Board members compensate for the Chair's weakness and speak up when problems occur, nothing gets done and frustration rises. With no sense of order in meetings, quiet members may not be able to speak up, thereby depriving the Board of their knowledge. Meetings run late and are unproductive. Effective Board members may find excuses to miss meetings and may eventually resign from the Board.

If the Chair allows motions that are ill advised or out of order, the Board could make flawed decisions or ones that contravene the legislation, bylaws, or policies and could therefore be deemed to be invalid.

## Intervention

Train your Chair to establish order, direction, and equal involvement at meetings. Teach him to deal with digressions, domination, verbal abuse, and other dysfunctions during meetings. Coach him to say no graciously but firmly, for the sake of a strong decision-making process.

Until the spineless Chair is trained to perform his duties effectively, Board members should not continue to suffer. Rather, they must act as co-owners of the process and speak up when the Chair does not address a damaging problem. They should not expect leadership to come solely from the Chair.

See Appendix D for tools for meeting Chairs and participants.

PROBLEM

# 48

# THE CHAIR WHO IS ATTACHED TO THE POSITION

The Chair of a Community Board has served for decades and repeatedly gets reelected, since her name is widely recognized across the community. Her reason for not stepping aside is that no one else wants the job. Actually, she is attached to the position and enjoys the attention and the public visibility that it gives her.

## Potential Damage

With few exceptions, individuals who remain in the same position for a long time tend to become stale and are much more likely to resist change and new ideas. In the case of a city and its Municipal Council, the organization's personality and the mayor's personality become one and the same. This may make it difficult for the Municipal Council to attract members with a fresh approach. Those who do join may soon become disillusioned and therefore operate at a fraction of their capacity.

## Intervention

Express appreciation to the Chair for her dedication and service, and then talk to her about succession planning and the community's need for fresh leadership. Have a pool of potential leaders who are engaged in the affairs of the community and will bring knowledge and commitment, so that a smooth transition can occur when the Chair finally steps aside. If she refuses to step aside, you may wish to launch a campaign to replace her with a well qualified individual at the next election.

In some organizations, the applicable legislation, bylaws, or policies limit the number of consecutive terms that the same individual can serve in the same position. If such term limits are to be established, the bylaws should stipulate how an exception can be made to them, so as to be able to retain an exceptionally talented individual in office.

P R O B L E M

# 49

## THE CHAIR WHO IS A POOR TEAM-BUILDER

This Chair is very knowledgeable and bright. He has creative and visionary ideas but does not connect very well with his Board. He dreams up great initiatives and promotes them to the community on his own, expressing impatience with his "unenlightened" colleagues and a sincere hope that they will finally see how smart his initiatives are and follow his lead. He never tries to build consensus among the Board members for his ideas nor does he attempt to build on their own ideas and suggestions.

## Potential Damage

Board members are likely to resent the Chair and find him condescending and disrespectful. They may refuse to follow his lead, not because the initiatives he proposes are flawed but because he does not involve them in identifying problems and formulating solutions. Levels of trust and respect may be eroded, and an adversarial environment may develop. Backroom conspiracies to undermine the Chair or have him removed will not be far behind.

## Intervention

Teach the Chair team-building skills. Suggest that he engage the Board in defining problems together and then identifying solutions. Until the Chair develops these skills, encourage Board members to avoid a defensive reaction to his ideas and be prepared to evaluate them based on merit and not on the Chair's team-building skills (or lack thereof). Board members should leave their egos behind and act this way for the sake of the community that they all serve.

# CHAPTER SEVEN

# DYSFUNCTIONAL BOARDS

Each Board has its own collective personality, that is, a set of dynamics, norms, acceptable behaviors, and related flaws. The key to the Board's success in providing quality leadership is in building Board strength and thereby reducing the frequency and severity of problems. This chapter focuses on problems that relate to the Board as a collective decision-making body.

See Appendix A for a Board Effectiveness Audit and Appendix B for Board Evaluation Tools.

# 50

# THE BOARD AS A SOCIAL CLUB

One Board functions as a social club. Individuals join it primarily to meet interesting people and make business contacts. Meetings are informal and unfocused, with jokes, gossip, and side stories shared throughout. Members look forward to the premeeting or postmeeting networking over alcoholic beverages. Most of the real work gets done by the CEO and the Board officers, and very little gets done by the other Board members. Meaningful questioning by Board members is rare. Members have a very low tolerance for arguments and disputes and are anxious to keep the peace and the smiles.

## Potential Damage

The expectation of a happy and social environment makes it difficult for conscientious Board members to raise tough questions or air dissenting views. This can make discussions superficial and shallow and can lead to flawed decisions that the Board may live to regret.

Leaving all the real work to the officers and the CEO makes the organization dependent on them and creates vulnerabilities if and when they leave. In addition, when the officers and the CEO do all the work, they can be tempted to take excessive risks or abuse their powers for personal gain or even fraud, since they doubt that the weak Board will ever scrutinize their actions in a meaningful way.

## Intervention

Establish that a Board is not a social club but a serious decision-making body. Stress that *there are no stupid questions, except those you don't ask or those that show that you did not read the premeeting materials.* Emphasize that spirited debates and conflicting views are not problems but signs of a healthy Board. Give members self-evaluation forms to complete at the end of every meeting (see Appendix B). Tell prospective Board members about the Board's functions and the duties of its members before they agree to consider serving on it.

## PROBLEM 51

## GROUPTHINK

A Board engages in "groupthink," being too comfortable with itself and too cozy with the CEO. It is detached and loses sight of its communities of citizens, shareholders, or stakeholders, or the Board takes them for granted.

On another Board, certain assumptions are so entrenched that few members dare to challenge them. Those who try are decisively stifled by condescending reactions or nasty body language. For example, when a new Board member dares to suggest that a rival organization might be approached for assistance or joint work, others rush to educate her in the way things are done: *"Smarten up. We don't make deals with the devil around here,"* or: *"You must be joking. How can you be so naive?"*

### Potential Damage

Groupthink distances the Board from the community that it serves, erodes its credibility, and makes the Board irrelevant. It diminishes the Board's capacity for free and independent thinking and stifles innovation and creativity. It entrenches the organization in the past and prevents the Board from abandoning outdated assumptions and mindsets. With groupthink, serious problems that have gone unchallenged for many years will persist. Effective leaders will find the Board unattractive to join or will leave it shortly after joining.

## Intervention

Emphasize the importance of creativity, innovation, and openness to new ideas, as well as the value of being connected to the community that the Board is mandated to serve. If you observe instinctive dismissal of ideas as nonstarters, remind members to hear people out before judging their ideas.

Try forcing the Board to experiment with new or even outrageous or unthinkable suggestions, so it stops being too cozy with itself and with what it considers to be sacred truth.

Search for confident and fresh new members to revitalize the Board. Develop initiatives to engage the Board in dialogue with its community on current issues.

PROBLEM

# 52

# PARTISAN POLITICS

A publicly elected Board has a tradition of functioning along political lines. Its members are divided into a *government party* and an *opposition party*. The government party controls the agenda, fights off the opposition, and constantly works to get reelected. The opposition party opposes and discredits the government party and continually works to defeat it in the next election.

## Potential Damage

Being constantly engaged in political combat, Board members are unlikely to listen to others with the intent of learning but rather with the intent of discrediting them and forming rebuttals. There is limited ability to benefit from ideas, since no one trusts the motivation of adversaries. With reelection prospects being foremost on people's minds, much needed initiatives may be abandoned because they might harm a party's reelection prospects. Conversely, flawed initiatives may be pursued because the pollsters say they are popular and will help the members win votes at election time.

With the factions being preoccupied with fighting each other, it is doubtful that they will be able to give the CEO coherent directions or hold him or her truly accountable. Worse yet, some may try to use the professional staff to help them discredit their opponents, thereby putting staff members in awkward situations and possibly causing them to contemplate new careers.

## Intervention

The fact that partisan politics have been your lot for a while does not mean that they cannot be abandoned. As a Board member with integrity and backbone, you can act as a catalyst for change. Remind your Board repeatedly of its fiduciary duties. Stress the need to set aside political differences for the sake of providing quality leadership to the staff and the community.

If such efforts are not forthcoming from within the Board, community groups or prominent citizens can demand that the Board stop playing partisan politics and start serving the community. Media coverage can be used to exert pressure and advance the goal of better government.

# 53

# TOO MANY SOLOISTS

A Board consists of entrepreneurs, law enforcement officers, or others who are used to making unilateral decisions and telling people what to do. Eager to get things done and impress the community, Board members compete with one another, promote their own initiatives, and propose their own motions during Board meetings. There is no sense of a collectively driven agenda or strategic direction. It feels like a choir of soloists who have no capacity to work as a team.

## Potential Damage

Board members become personally and emotionally attached to their own ideas, while their colleagues feel ambushed by unannounced or unexplained proposals. In an effort to obtain a majority for their own proposals, Board members may employ unprincipled tactics such as vote trading. Egos get bruised when individuals lose. Staff members who implement Board orders do not know what to expect next and where the next idea will come from. The community is confused since its needs are interpreted differently by each Board member.

## Intervention

Teach your Board to balance independent initiative with teamwork. Start by convening a planning session for the Board to jointly develop a prioritized strategic plan, with advice from the CEO and professional staff and advisers and with input from the community. Then direct the CEO to prepare implementation schedules and budgets. The Board's role will then be to collectively oversee the plan's implementation and give directions to the CEO. Motions will be prewritten by Board committees or staff to advance the collectively adopted strategic plan.

## PROBLEM
# 54
## PARALYZED BY FEAR

On one Board, debate on an issue is dominated by fear that a particular decision may offend a powerful group or prominent individual or even cause those offended to retaliate. On a different Board, several lawyers are advising the Board on minimizing legal exposure, and the Board becomes frightened and extremely restricted in the range of options that it considers. Paralysis sets in.

### Potential Damage

The math is simple: Spending a great deal of time and energy speculating on worst-case scenarios leaves less time and energy for creating positive outcomes. The Board can then lose control over the organization's agenda to fear and speculation. It may be hampered from considering creative (albeit not risk-free) ways of addressing controversial issues.

### Intervention

Refocus the discussion on what the Board actually wants to achieve, and only then discuss how to minimize risk. Try this script: *"Can we focus for a while on what we want to achieve here and what the community needs from us? Afterwards, we can talk about how to implement the ideas and how we might prevent bad outcomes and minimize legal exposure."*

# 55
## DRIVEN BY RIVALRY

A corporation's Board decides to open a new branch in a small community, mainly because of rumors that its chief rival plans to do the same. Debates are driven by the Board's collective sense of pride, a desire to always be first, and an unstated urge to retaliate for past grievances with the competitor. Although the business case for the new branch is not compelling, the Board clings to signs in favor of opening the branch, even those only remotely positive.

## Potential Damage

Without a solid business case, the new branch may flounder or fail, and this is too high a price to pay for pride and the satisfaction of exacting revenge. If and when it becomes clear that there isn't enough business to sustain the new branch, the Board may choose to persist and refuse to close the branch for fear that the Board might be discredited and be deemed to have lost to its rival once again. The ultimate victim of this tit-for-tat rivalry is the corporation itself.

## Intervention

Insist that Board decisions be based on solid business cases and that the Board resist being distracted by side issues such as rivalry, anger, or desire for revenge. Develop a Board culture where egos are parked outside, and economic viability and excellent customer service always come first.

PROBLEM

# 56

# SHORTSIGHTED PREOCCUPATION WITH MONEY

A locally based community services organization receives a pitch from a philanthropist: *"I'll donate up to $100,000 to match any funds that you raise on your own."* The Board gets excited, springs into action immediately, and focuses most staff and volunteer efforts on raising money.

In another setting, a philanthropist donates money on the condition that it be used for projects that are marginal to the organization's core mandate or are not current priorities. He is assertive and definitive, and the Board acquiesces. After all, who can argue with money?

## Potential Damage

The organization's agenda is hijacked by a shortsighted focus on money. Staff and volunteers are distracted from the core mandate, and the focus on serving community clients is diluted. With reduced service levels, client frustration grows and the organization's credibility suffers. In the case where the Board gives in and concentrates on the philanthropist's projects, attention is diverted from the Board's strategic plan.

## Intervention

Resist the temptation to pursue anything and everything that smells of money. Insist that the Board be driven first and foremost by its core mandate, vision, and strategic plan. Yes, raising money may be important, but financial goals are more likely to be achieved and sustained with a happy and satisfied community of clients.

If a philanthropist places conditions on a proposed donation, meet him or her in person, review the organization's strategic priorities, and negotiate an appropriate use for the funds. But capitulating to such a donor's demands would be misguided and inappropriate.

PROBLEM

# 57

# THE ADVERSARIAL BOARD

On an adversarial Board, decisions are routinely made on the basis of a narrow majority. When the full Board is in attendance and voting on a motion that is sponsored by the majority, the numbers are usually five votes in favor and four votes against. Minority-sponsored motions are defeated by a vote of four in favor and five against. Winning usually means that the other side loses.

## Potential Damage

Although parliamentary procedure requires only a majority vote to adopt a motion, chronic narrow majorities indicate an adversarial Board, in which factions advance their own causes and refuse to listen to and genuinely learn from others. These dynamics tend to limit the scope of debates and reduce the likelihood of balanced decisions that accommodate all legitimate interests. The community then loses the holistic and thoughtful leadership that it deserves.

As another consequence, if a motion passes by a narrow majority, it is possible that it would be rescinded at the next meeting if several members of the majority are absent. In such a setting, no one can afford to be sick or go on vacation, for fear of an ambush in their absence.

### Intervention

Despite adversarial dynamics, the Board should consider shifting away—at least partly—from a *"you against me"* mentality to *"you and me against the problem."* Factions should agree on when they will work on a purely divided ideological basis and when they will work as a team. To achieve this goal, schedule a Board planning session, probably under the guidance of an impartial facilitator. Discuss common and diverging goals and how the Board can fulfill its duties to the community in a positive and collaborative manner.

PROBLEM

# 58

## POST-DECISION ATTACKS

After a Board decision is made, a member who voted against it mounts a public campaign to discredit the Board, undermine the implementation of the decision, and build public pressure to have it revisited at a subsequent Board meeting.

### Potential Damage

Trust and respect among Board members are eroded, and deep resentments may develop. Confronted by public pressure, the Board may capitulate and rescind or dilute its decision, even if it would be beneficial to the community over the long term. This is bound to weaken the Board and diminish its ability to make tough but necessary decisions. It could also make the Board susceptible to bullying by individuals or groups, sometimes at the expense of the larger community.

### Intervention

There are times when unanimity is not achievable, and a formal vote is needed to bring an issue to closure. In such cases, there will be a winning side and a losing side. However, it should be clarified to the Board that once a decision is made, it is no longer a majority decision. It is a Board decision, and the minority is duty-bound to accept it as a legitimate collective decision and move on. This principle is often referred to as the *solidarity rule*. The principle is not as absolute as some people believe, and the following points should be considered:

- The solidarity rule is more of an expectation than an enforceable rule. With freedom of expression laws, it is questionable whether a Board can actually muzzle its dissenting members or punish them for speaking against a validly made Board decision, unless such disciplinary measures are clearly spelled out in legislation, bylaws, or policies.

- Some people expect a member who voted in the minority to actively endorse the Board's decision, rather than merely accept it as a legitimate collective outcome. This expectation is unrealistic, since it may require someone to make dishonest statements of support. Holding a dissenting view (even after a decision is made) is a fundamental right in a democracy, and it would be unfair and inappropriate to tamper with it.

- Questions are often raised about how those who voted against a motion should respond to questions from the media or the public. Consider this response: *"There are two parts to my answer. First, as to my vote, it is a matter of public record. I voted against this motion. Having said this, I need to clarify that, in a democracy, the minority must be heard—and my views were heard—but it is the majority that rules. It is my duty as a Board member to accept the outcome and move on to other issues."*

- If, subsequent to a decision, a Board member becomes aware of significant new information that necessitates revisiting it, she may initiate a motion to rescind or amend the motion (provided it had not been fully implemented). Board members should not use the revisiting option petulantly or for manipulative purposes.

■ The solidarity rule does not always apply. One exception is when a Board does not have the power to finalize a particular decision but only to make a recommendation to the members or shareholders (when they have the ultimate say on an issue). In such cases, it is legitimate for dissenting Board members to speak as members or shareholders and apprise others of their dissenting views before the vote on the Board's recommendation.

■ The Board should also consider that it is difficult to enforce the solidarity rule and that it may be hard for dissenters to follow it if their views were marginalized, silenced, or ignored by an aggressive and arrogant majority. If all members are listened to and treated with respect, violations of the solidarity rule will be minimized.

PROBLEM

# 59

## THE INDECISIVE BOARD

A Board has a hard time making decisions, especially when issues seem contentious. It routinely postpones or tables motions or refers them to staff or committees for more studies. It pursues a never-ending quest for compromises and unanimity and has a reputation for revisiting decisions when confronted by vocal opposition.

### Potential Damage

The community and the staff may become frustrated by not receiving clear and reliable directions. Contractors may be uncertain if they can expect a decision to be implemented. Vocal community groups may take advantage of the indecision, fight the Board, and successfully block an initiative they don't like. Their efforts may succeed even if the initiative is very necessary.

## Intervention

Encourage your Board to balance the need for caution with the need to be decisive and take calculated risks in a timely fashion. The community does not expect decisions that please everyone or ones that are perfect in every way, as long as the community is kept informed of the complexity of issues and the reasons for choosing certain initiatives. Discourage the reversal of necessary decisions solely on the basis that vocal minorities object to them.

PROBLEM
60

## THE BOARD THAT NEVER TURNS BACK

A Board is determined to have its decisions fully implemented, regardless of problems that surface after they are made. Members have no patience for those who discover flaws in a decision, commonly telling them: *"You should have said it then. It's too late now. We're forging ahead. There is no going back."* Sometimes it's a matter of pride, and the Board may desperately seek real or manufactured data to validate hanging on to a flawed decision.

## Potential Damage

A flawed decision may be fully implemented, thereby potentially damaging the organization and wasting money and other resources. The culture of not going back is bound to have a stifling effect: Those who discover problems with a decision may not speak up, since they believe it is futile to pursue the issue with such a stubborn Board.

## Intervention

Emphasize to the Board that decisiveness and speed should never be its only goals. It is clearly not wise to start or continue the implementation of flawed decisions just for the sake of maintaining an image of an unwavering Board. At times, the Board will be duty-bound to swallow its pride and abandon, modify, or reduce the scope of a bad initiative.

To reduce the likelihood of flawed decisions that need revisiting, ensure that all necessary research and analysis are done and that potential risks and problems are taken into account before making a decision. In short, the Board should take its time and refuse to rush its decisions. However, the Board should be prepared to go back should it prove necessary.

PROBLEM
61

## KEEPING THEM IN THE DARK

Anticipating opposition to a contentious proposal, the proponents of the motion keep other Board members in the dark about the details until the meeting, with the strategy of preventing them from plotting to defeat the proposal. As another strategic step, the proposal is scheduled late in the meeting, when key critics may have left and others may be too tired to oppose it.

## Potential Damage

This deceptive strategy is bound to insult Board members, erode trust, and build resentment. It may also backfire and increase opposition to a positive and much needed initiative. In addition, it may encourage other Board members to invent their own deceptive strategies to advance their own goals. With an adversarial culture developing, members may become less focused on the ideas presented and more focused on undermining their presenters.

## Intervention

Have a discussion with the Board about its working culture. Demand zero tolerance for manipulative tactics, and give direct feedback to those who practice them. Explain that shared decision making means that all members must have access to the same information early, so a proposal can be evaluated on its merits rather than on its proponent's political skill.

PROBLEM

# 62

## NITPICKING OVER SMALL DETAILS

A Board is populated by detail-oriented members who nitpick at small details and have no tolerance for minor ambiguities. They routinely speculate on every remote eventuality and try to define exact details of how decisions will be implemented. In one setting, such a Board takes up valuable meeting time to collectively edit a letter requesting government funding. In another setting, the Board appoints a committee or task force and then defines not only what the committee must achieve but also whom it will approach and what data it will consider.

## Potential Damage

In its quest for perfection and fixation on minutiae, the Board may lose sight of broad directions and overall outcomes. Attempts to eliminate small ambiguities are tiring, time-consuming, and frustrating, and several people may tune out and stop listening. In addition, with nothing left undefined, those charged with implementing decisions will have no latitude or discretion to tackle unanticipated problems or circumstances.

## Intervention

Discourage the practice of nitpicking and vying for perfection. Suggest that although the Board would want its motions to be clear, it should focus more of its efforts on the *why* and the *what* and less on the *how*, the *when*, and the *where*. Suggest as well that the Board develop some comfort with ambiguity in the minor details, as long as the overall intent is abundantly clear.

Alternatively, encourage the practice of preparing decision-making options or motions before a meeting, with broad aspects clearly defined in written form. This will likely increase the Board's comfort with the wording of proposals and reduce nitpicking at the meeting.

PROBLEM

# 63
## DEFERRING TO EXPERIENCE

When encountering contentious decisions or ones they don't understand, most members of a Board defer to the Chair, to experienced or assertive members, or to the CEO. Some Board members routinely say: *"I'll go with whatever everyone else wants to do."*

## Potential Damage

With most Board members deferring to experienced colleagues or the CEO, the real initiative and leadership are in the hands of only a few people, and collective strength does not develop. The Board becomes dependent on experienced individuals and may become very weak when they leave. In addition, flawed proposals may be approved not on their merits but because the originators are respected, assertive, or hold positions of authority.

## Intervention

Press individuals to share their views, despite their readiness to acquiesce and go with the flow. Stress that each member is an equal partner in decision making and that a chain is only as strong as its weakest link. Encourage debate and celebrate diversity of opinions.

PROBLEM

# 64

## COLLECTIVE IMPATIENCE

A Board has a tradition of generating quick decisions and has no tolerance for slower and more measured processes. Meetings are like a fast-moving train: *"Let's get on with this decision. It's time to walk the talk. We need to be good leaders and act decisively."* As an added twist, some Board members take bets on how quickly the meeting will end. The Chair's greatest pride is in the shortness of a meeting and the volume of decisions that it generates.

## Potential Damage

Cautious Board members may remain silent for fear of offending the tradition of efficiency. Valid concerns may go unexpressed, and risk levels may rise. Knowing the expectation of expediency, the CEO and professional staff may be afraid to request time to study an issue more carefully. They may therefore answer Board questions on the fly and offer quick fixes that generate short-term gains but potentially long-term pains for the organization.

## Intervention

Someone (possibly you?) must find the strength to resist the pressure to make flawed decisions quickly. If a Board's primary focus is on expediency, the victim may be the organization. So don't be afraid to say: *"At the risk of being unpopular, the desire to move quickly is laudable, but generating quick solutions for complex problems could come back to haunt us later. I suggest we slow down and give the issues the attention they need."*

PROBLEM

# 65

# PREDETERMINED OUTCOMES

When dealing with contentious issues, members of a Board form alliances and trade votes in advance of a meeting, to rally support and ensure that their proposals win. In another setting, Board members who made promises at election time believe they must honor them. At meetings, there isn't much debate since most people already know how they'll vote. All they worry about is how the undecided vote (that of the principled and honest members who want to learn from the discussion and who refuse to make deals before the meeting) will turn out.

## Potential Damage

If outcomes are predetermined, meetings and discussions are meaningless. Minds are closed and members are not interested in learning. In such settings, decision making is usually limited to two options: Either a motion will be passed or it will be defeated.

This may preclude the adoption of a better third option that may deliver greater benefits and lower risks to the organization. In addition, predetermined outcomes may cause the community to become cynical, with its confidence and trust in the Board diminishing. Last, a Board decision may end up being challenged in court and possibly overturned on the basis that minds were closed when the meeting began.

## Intervention

Establish during Board orientation that members must come to meetings with open minds and listen and learn from the views presented, regardless of any premade promises and regardless of whether they like or dislike the presenters of certain views. Emphasize that closed minds present a risk to the organization.

If you become aware of this problem at a meeting, speak up: *"Can I say something? I am getting a feeling that for some people, the outcomes of this meeting are all but final. If this is true, it will taint our decision-making process and cast doubt on our credibility as a Board. With all due respect, I believe our citizens need us to park our biases at the door, commit to learning from the discussion, and make informed and balanced decisions on their behalf."*

# CHAPTER EIGHT

# UNPRODUCTIVE BOARD MEETINGS

Most interactions among Board members occur during meetings, some being face-to-face meetings and others being virtual meetings (teleconferences, videoconferences, e-meetings, and discussions via e-mail). This chapter discusses Board meeting problems. See Appendix B for evaluation tools for meetings.

PROBLEM
## 66
## NO CLEAR PURPOSE TO A MEETING

Members do not know why a meeting was called, what it is supposed to accomplish, why they were invited, and how they can help make it successful. The agenda is nonexistent or too sparse or—conversely—contains far too many items to be completed within the available time. In addition, individuals who hold significant knowledge or clout are not present at the meeting.

## Potential Damage

Prevailing wisdom suggests that *if you don't know where you're going, any road will take you there.* If a meeting is poorly planned, members will be confused and may question why they had to disrupt their schedules to attend it. A packed agenda makes it difficult to focus the meeting on key issues and give them the time and attention they need. If individuals with knowledge and clout are absent, progress will be stalled and it will be difficult to make quality decisions.

## Intervention

If there is no purpose in holding a meeting that has been called, it may be okay to cancel it. If there is a purpose, it should be clarified in the meeting's notice and further explained at the start of the meeting. If the Chair does not delineate the purpose and the desired outcomes, members should insist that this be done at the start. If in the course of a meeting it becomes evident that meaningful progress cannot be made, it is okay to end the suffering and adjourn the meeting.

Next time, establish the meeting's purpose and desired outcomes and make sure that individuals with the necessary knowledge and clout are invited and know how important it is that they attend. Plan a realistic agenda that is neither sparse nor packed. To avoid a packed agenda, delegate some items to committees or management and postpone items that can wait. Feel free to drop agenda items that are not likely to lead to productive interactions. Deal with less important items in teleconference calls or e-meetings.

# 67

## CHAOTIC, DISORDERLY MEETINGS

No rules for speaking are established at a certain meeting, or the rules are not followed. Board members speak whenever they want and do not wait for the Chair to recognize them when their turns come. They often interrupt others in midsentence. Several Board members speak simultaneously, with the louder and more assertive members frequently prevailing.

### Potential Damage

The decision-making process is chaotic and disorganized. Good ideas are lost or not fully explored, which erodes the Board's ability to make quality decisions in a measured and organized manner. Louder and more assertive members dictate the pace and direction of the meeting. Quiet members are pushed aside, along with their knowledge and ideas.

### Intervention

Many Boards rely on rules of order (also referred to as parliamentary procedure) in their meetings. Rules of order are generally intended to help facilitate progress and engage members in debate and decision making on an equal basis, while protecting fundamental rights. However, strict reliance on these rules can stifle and constrain debates and may therefore achieve the opposite results from which they are intended.

To ensure order and fairness, establish basic rules of order for meetings: *"Please speak after being recognized by the Chair, make your comments brief, make room for other people to share their ideas, and focus on issues, not people."* Establish commitment to the rules and stress that it is okay to complain if they are not followed. Give members sample intervention scripts for use if and when needed (see Appendix D).

### Practical Tips for Using Rules of Order

■ Under parliamentary procedure, decisions can be made formally, via motions, which are usually moved, seconded, debated, and then voted on. It is important that motions be concise, complete, and unambiguous. Motions should be written down before they are considered. Draft motions should be circulated before a meeting so Board members can prepare for well-focused debates and informed decisions.

■ It is best to avoid making a motion until there is a full understanding of the problem that needs to be solved. If a motion is presented prematurely, the Chair or another member may ask the mover to delay "solution-mode" until the actual problem has been defined. If the proponent persists, the group should not hesitate to vote to postpone the motion or refer it to a designated committee or professional staff for assessment.

■ Under parliamentary procedure, the wording of motions may be changed via amendments. Traditionally, an amendment is formally introduced, debated, and then voted on. The Board then returns to the main motion (original or amended). This process may work well in adversarial settings or large meetings, but it can be rigid and cumbersome for smaller Boards. A less formal and more flexible approach is often much more productive.

■ A decision that was not fully implemented can usually be rescinded or modified by the Board at a subsequent meeting.

■ See Appendix C for myths and truths about rules of order.

# 68

# STUFFINESS AND FORMALITY

The members of a corporation's Board speak, act, and dress very formally, and meetings have an air of stuffiness. People always stand when they want to speak. They use formal language and strict parliamentary procedure, even if a meeting is small. No one smiles and Board work seems very serious, even when insignificant issues are being discussed.

## Potential Damage

The excessive formality stifles creativity and precludes spontaneity, humanity, and a light touch. The overly structured interactions restrict the Board's leeway to fully explore ideas in an informal and flexible manner. Meetings move along in a strict and linear fashion, and progress is slow. The rigidity makes it difficult to back away from a bad idea after debate begins. The excessive formality may deter effective individuals from joining the Board.

## Intervention

Welcome your Board to the twenty-first century. Compliment members on their discipline, and then explain the damaging effects of excessive formality. Gradually introduce small changes to deformalize and humanize Board meetings, while retaining the positive aspects of established customs. Try lightening things up via team-building activities.

PROBLEM

# 69

## TIME WASTING

Members regularly arrive late, and the Chair decides to delay the starting time of the meeting until all of the members are present. During the meeting, some members are long-winded and give extended and confusing preambles to their main points. Others repeat points already made by their colleagues. Yet others digress from the agenda and discuss side issues or personal stories. These behaviors make the meeting slow, long, and monotonous.

### Potential Damage

With time being wasted, less time is available for quality discussion and consensus building. Members get frustrated and bored and tune out. They may stop listening, even when the discussion is relevant to decision making. The lost time means having to rush through subsequent agenda items without careful scrutiny, thereby risking flawed decisions.

### Intervention

Start meetings on time, even if all members are not there (provided that enough members are present to meet the quorum requirement). Maintain a comfortable yet steady pace throughout the meeting. Institute token rewards for behaviors that help manage time effectively. Consider symbolic fun penalties for late arrivals and for other time-wasting behaviors.

Use the following scripts to deal with specific causes of wasted time:

- In case of rambling, interrupt with: *"George, we need to pick up the pace,"* or: *"Sherry, our time is running short and we have several people waiting to speak. Can you please wrap it up?"*

- In case of repetition, try this: *"Members, we are behind in our schedule. Does anyone have anything new to add, and—if not— shall we proceed to the vote?"*

- In case of digressions, try this: *"Can we please get back to the agenda?"* or: *"We need to focus on the core issue, which is* ————.*"* (A word of caution: Some digressions may provide much needed downtime during a heavy agenda, so don't be compulsive about enforcing the rules.)

As a preventive measure, you may open a meeting by encouraging members to be focused and concise, avoid unnecessary repetition, and remain on track. In a large or contentious meeting, it may be productive to formally set time limits, such as two minutes per person; give a "one minute left" warning, then a 30-second warning, and then an indication that time is up.

Last, offer training to members or give them feedback privately to help them speak and/or listen effectively. Videotaping and playback of comments can provide eye-opening feedback.

PROBLEM

# 70

## DEADLOCK

An agenda item proves to be complex and tricky, or it is controversial and the Board is polarized on it. Discussion is going in circles and no progress is made. The Board is deadlocked.

## Potential Damage

Board members get tired and frustrated. If and when the next agenda item is reached, there will be less time available for it, and members may not be fresh and capable of giving it the care and attention that it needs, thereby risking rushed and possibly flawed decisions.

## Intervention

Call a break and suggest that members go for a walk or engage in some physical activity to get refreshed and increase their capacity for creativity and new ideas.

As a different option, if the Board is polarized between Position A and Position B, you could try this: Ask members to break into small working groups, with advocates of both positions represented in each group. The advocates of Position A will articulate Position B with some passion, and they will then receive feedback on whether they fully heard and understood Position B. Then the roles will be reversed. As a result of this exercise, members may discover how poorly they were listening to one another.

If the decision on a deadlocked item can wait, the item can be delegated to a task force made up of holders of different or conflicting views, with a direction to present consensus at the next meeting.

PROBLEM

71

## SIDE CONVERSATIONS

Two Board members conduct a loud and distracting side conversation in the middle of a meeting.

## Potential Damage

This behavior distracts and annoys other members. In addition, the parties to the side conversation are not listening and learning from the general discussion, and their ability to make informed decisions will be reduced. Later, when it comes time to vote, they may be too embarrassed to request an update and may vote without understanding the issues.

## Intervention

Pause the meeting and check the reason for the side conversation. If it is legitimate, wait until things settle down and then resume the general discussion. If not, try this: *"Heather and Mike. We need your attention."* Then ask the person who was interrupted to continue.

Alternatively, speak to repeat offenders privately after the meeting. Your intervention need not be negative or scolding. Just give the individuals feedback and remind them that the Board and the community they care about need them to be engaged in debate and decision making.

Yet another approach is to make the meeting so dynamic, interesting, and interactive that side conversations will become unlikely.

PROBLEM
72

## ELECTRONIC DISTRACTIONS

Some Board members use computers or other electronic devices not only to view meeting-related documents electronically but also to browse the Internet or respond to their e-mails or text messages while the meeting is in progress.

## Potential Damage

These Board members are distracted, and their ability to listen and learn from discussions and make informed decisions is compromised. They may also be slow to contribute their input, which can lead to flawed decisions. Things get worse if a computer or other electronic device malfunctions and its user tries to fix it, becoming even more distracted.

## Intervention

Discuss with the Board the duty to pay attention to discussions, and explain the damaging effects of electronic distractions. As a preventive measure, pick up the pace of the meeting and make it more interactive, so members will be less likely to be tempted by side activities.

PROBLEM

# 73

# SLEEPING DURING A MEETING

A Board member falls asleep during a meeting.

## Potential Damage

The sleeping Board member is obviously not positioned to make informed decisions or contribute his ideas to the discussions. Moreover, other members may be distracted or embarrassed for their sleeping colleague.

## Intervention

Call a fitness break or ask members to go for a walk in the fresh air or the rain. When they break up, you could approach the individual and – if he is still asleep—wake him up and see if something can be done to increase his alertness. After the break, pick up the pace of the meeting.

As a preventive measure, plan varied activities beyond just sitting down and being lectured to, especially if the meeting is lengthy. Schedule breaks at least every two hours. In addition, try asking individuals for input even when they do not ask to speak (thereby perpetuating an expectation that they act as partners in decision making). Last, avoid sleep-inducing heavy meals or alcoholic beverages before and during meetings.

## PROBLEM
# 74
# PARKING LOT CONVERSATIONS

Some Board members are quiet during meetings, but they engage in spirited discussions during breaks or in the parking lot after the meeting. Such conversations may include criticisms of decisions that were made and complaints about how the meeting was run.

### Potential Damage

Relevant concerns are expressed when it is too late for them to affect Board decisions and, as a result, the organization may be at risk. Unexpressed concerns about flaws in the conduct of meetings perpetuate and legitimize dysfunctional practices.

### Intervention

If the relevant information was shared during a break and you become aware of it, bring it to everyone's attention when the meeting resumes. If the ideas were shared after the meeting was adjourned, it may be necessary to revisit a flawed decision at a subsequent meeting.

As a preventive measure, establish that *there are no stupid ques-*

*tions or comments, except those that you keep to yourself.* Remind members that a Board is not a social club but a serious decision-making body, and that they are negligent in their duty to the organization when they do not share important observations or withhold them until after the meeting.

## FULL-SCALE E-MAIL WAR

A nasty argument flares up between two Board members after a meeting. To ensure that everyone is aware of the righteousness of her cause, one of the combatants sends a nasty e-mail to her rival, copying it to all Board members. Others jump into the fray and a full-scale e-mail war erupts, with people making offensive remarks that they would never say face-to-face.

### Potential Damage

A seemingly small argument can become an ugly and irreconcilable dispute, poisoning the air and destroying team spirit. The Board may become fractured and lose its capacity to work as a cohesive unit and direct its full attention to its core mandate. Some people may regret what they wrote, but it may be too late to withdraw it. In a public body, e-mails may be subject to access to information requests, and the matter can become a major public embarrassment.

### Intervention

Educate the Board that e-mail is best used to share information and exchange ideas, but that disputes are better resolved in face-to-face meetings. Encourage Board members to think carefully before clicking on the *Reply All* and *Send* buttons, especially when the message expresses anger or frustration. Remind Board members that e-mail transmissions may not be secure and private. Ask them to pause before pushing the *Send* button and consider whether they would be comfortable having the media obtain a poisonous e-mail (under access to information laws or by being leaked by a recipient), which could then become the subject of highly damaging news coverage.

PROBLEM

# 76

## WASTEFUL TELECONFERENCE CALL

There are many participants in a teleconference call. People interject whenever they want, and no one knows who is speaking. Assertive members dominate, and quiet members are left behind. Some members tune out to check their e-mail, and no one can tell that they are no longer logged in to the teleconference call. Some people are inadvertently disconnected, and some hang up in frustration.

### Potential Damage

There is a risk that nothing will be accomplished during such a teleconference call, that the investment of time and money in the call will be wasted, and that people will find excuses to avoid such calls in the future.

### Intervention

If possible, keep the number of participants in the call to a minimum, ideally no more than eight (except that if the Board is larger than eight, all Board members will need to be involved).

Ask participants to give their full attention to the call and avoid distractions, such as checking unrelated e-mails or engaging in other conversations. Make the call short, keep a dynamic pace, and ask members to keep their comments brief.

At the beginning of the call, explain how people will identify themselves and get permission to speak (e.g., by calling out their name and having the Chair add it to the speaker's lineup), and then stick to this protocol. Check regularly with those who have not spoken to engage them in the discussion and determine whether they were inadvertently dropped from the call.

Limit teleconference calls to urgent decisions that cannot wait until the next face-to-face meeting. You may also choose to use teleconferences to handle housekeeping matters that do not require face-to-face interactions. However, discussions and decisions over sensitive or complex issues should be delayed until the next face-to-face meeting.

It may be prudent to confirm that your applicable legislation or bylaws permit the making of Board decisions by teleconference calls. If not, decisions made by teleconference call or any electronic means will need to be ratified at the next face-to-face Board meeting.

PROBLEM

# 77

## LOGISTICAL PROBLEMS

A meeting is plagued with logistical difficulties. The room is too hot or too cold. There is a lively and noisy event in the room next door. Computers, projectors, and microphones are malfunctioning. Refreshments and meals arrive late, and hot beverages are lukewarm. Members who requested vegetarian meals receive steaks or chicken sandwiches. In another setting, heavy meals and alcohol are served at Board meetings, with the goal of rewarding

Board members or putting them in a good mood. Unfortunately, this may backfire.

## Potential Damage

Logistical difficulties annoy and distract members and may reduce their ability to fully concentrate on the issues at hand and the decisions they need to make. In addition, excessive food and alcohol may make participants sleepy and incapable of remaining focused and alert. Alcohol has a tendency to release inhibitions and may cause Board members to do or say inappropriate things. Also, drinking alcohol could potentially endanger members as they drive home, which might lead to action taken against the organization in the event of an accident related to intoxication.

## Intervention

Logistical difficulties are best prevented through proactive planning. Ensure that your Board's executive assistant is aware of your needs and arranges for logistical support, thereby freeing the Board to give its full attention to the issues at hand. As a general rule, alcohol should not be allowed in conjunction with Board meetings.

## CHAPTER NINE

# FLAWED INTERACTIONS WITH MANAGEMENT

To ensure that its decisions are financially, technically, operationally, and legally sound, the Board must rely on advice from its Chief Executive Officer (CEO), professional staff, and external advisers. The Board should demand expert advice, prepared with objectivity and professionalism and untainted by political considerations. The Board should also require that the CEO create a safe working environment that encourages the staff to excel.

Everyone on the Board should be knowledgeable about the CEO's role and responsibilities. The CEO is responsible for implementing Board policies and strategic priorities and for providing the Board with professional expertise and decision-making support. The CEO also provides leadership to the management and staff team. The actual title of the CEO can vary from organization to organization, such as: General Manager, Chief Administrative

Officer, Executive Director, Chief Operating Officer, and Superintendent of Schools.

To be most effective, a CEO should have the following traits:

- Commitment and passion for the organization

- Knowledge of the organization's mandate and strategic priorities

- Familiarity with the applicable legislation, bylaws, and policies

- Knowledge of the strengths and weaknesses of the Board and the staff

- Effective articulation and exceptional listening skills

- People-building, relationship-building, and team-building skills

- Ability to give and receive constructive feedback

- Effective administrative and risk management skills

- Consistency, reliability, and accessibility

- Humility, openness, and eagerness to learn

- Honesty, integrity, and a principle-based approach

- Commitment to excellence

A Board is usually expected to focus primarily on policies, strategic priorities, and CEO oversight, and it should delegate the daily leadership and operational duties to the CEO. However, if an organization has less staff (or none), the Board needs to be more hands-on.

With a policy-focused Board, there are several principles that should govern the relationship and interactions between the Board and the CEO:

- A policy-focused Board directs most of its efforts on the organization's mission, vision, and strategic goals, while the

CEO focuses on implementing Board policies. The Board should establish what decisions constitute policy matters versus operational matters.

■ The Board should generally act as though it has only one employee: the CEO. In turn, the CEO should be accountable to and should generally take directions from the Board as a collective entity, not from individual Board members.

■ Staff members should be accountable to and take directions from the CEO or their own managers, going through the established chain of command. They should generally not receive directions from the Board or from individual Board members, although they may be required to be in communication with them.

■ Outside Board meetings, a Board member has no more authority than any individual from the community, except when that Board member has been delegated certain duties or powers by the Board. Individual Board members must not interfere with the work of staff members or bully or harass them.

■ Although the above principles are applicable when the CEO is trusted and respected, they may need to be abandoned when the CEO's competence is in doubt or when the CEO is not trusted or respected. In such cases, the Board may be duty-bound to take a more hands-on position, or else it will be negligent in performing its fiduciary duties to the organization.

## PROBLEM
# 78
## MICROMANAGEMENT

The Board of a large corporation insists on making operational decisions, such as choosing the color of the walls and tiles in a new office, the length of staff coffee breaks, and the words that staff members must use to greet customers. In another setting, a Board member hears a rumor about a staff member's improprieties and introduces a motion at a Board meeting that he be disciplined.

## Potential Damage

Micromanagement is likely to distract the Board from its primary tasks of monitoring the organization's mission, vision, and strategic goals and providing high-level oversight to the CEO. Micromanagement is bound to frustrate the CEO and may curtail her ability to use professional judgment to optimize results. Eventually, micromanagement by the Board may lead to the CEO's resignation.

## Intervention

If your organization is small and does not have substantial staff resources, micromanagement may be a reality that you must accept. However, if the Board has sufficient staff support, you may want to suggest that Board members focus on the *why* and the *what*, and leave it to the CEO to focus on the *how*, the *when*, and the *where*. Staff performance issues should generally be addressed by the CEO. The Board should get involved only in setting human resources policies or if the CEO fails to provide effective leadership to the staff.

If the above interventions are not forthcoming from the Board, the CEO should speak up in defense of effective governance and against micromanagement: *"May I suggest that you tell me what needs to be done and then allow me to figure out how?"* An analogy to consider is that the Board should remain on the balcony while the CEO manages from the ground floor.

PROBLEM

# 79

# PHYSICAL LABOR WITHOUT INSURANCE COVERAGE

In order to save an organization some money, one Board member who is a tradesman volunteers to repair equipment and machinery or do some renovations around the office. In another setting, volunteer Board members assist hired staff in preparing and serving food and in cleaning up after the group's annual banquet.

## Potential Damage

Board members who do physical labor without the proper insurance coverage place the organization at risk in the event of accidents on the job. The immediate savings would be quickly offset or substantially exceeded by the cost of a lawsuit or liability claim.

## Intervention

Refuse to allow volunteers to do physical labor unless you first obtain insurance coverage for them. A consultation with a lawyer and an insurance expert will help you reduce risk.

PROBLEM

# 80

## VIOLATING THE CHAIN OF COMMAND

Some members of a Board routinely roam the organization's offices and give directions to individual staff members. Sometimes there is an implied threat that refusing to follow a Board member's order can be a career-limiting move. In another setting, a Board member makes his own public pronouncements, suggesting that a certain staff member will soon be removed.

### Potential Damage

Board incursions into staff territory are bound to confuse, frustrate, and demoralize staff and curtail their ability to perform to their best. Staff members are unsure who their boss is: the CEO (or a designated manager), the Board as a whole, or individual Board members. This can distract staff from their work or cause them to perform at a fraction of their capacity. It can also lead to resignations and costly recruitment processes to replace those who leave. In extreme cases, it may lead staff members to take court action on charges of interference, bullying, and harassment.

### Intervention

Emphasize that the Board must generally act as a high-level governing body and operate as though it has only one employee, the CEO, who—in turn—has only one boss: the Board as a collective entity. Consequently, each staff member should generally have only one boss: the CEO or a designated manager. Although staff members may need to communicate with Board members as part of their work, they should receive directions primarily through the CEO.

As an extra measure, reassure staff members that it is safe for them to say no to a demanding Board member and that they will suffer no consequences for doing so. Encourage them to complain to the CEO or to a Board-designated liaison if such problems persist.

PROBLEM
# 81
## PUBLIC INSULTS OF STAFF MEMBERS

At a public meeting, a Board member or a citizen speaking to the Board implies that a staff member is negligent, incompetent, or dishonest. Not being a voting member, the staff member does not have the right to speak and therefore has no opportunity to set the record straight.

### Potential Damage

Tolerating attacks on staff members during public meetings is equivalent to allowing such staff members to be tried, judged, and punished without due process or opportunities to defend themselves. Staff members who are publicly attacked become demoralized and may therefore function at a fraction of their capacity. In the future, some of them may take the safe yet unprincipled route of trying hard to not offend abusive Board members or assertive citizens. They may even withhold contentious but essential details for fear of reprisals. Ultimately, effective staff members may resign, with the organization bearing the cost of recruiting and training their successors. Some angry staff members may pursue harassment charges against the Board, diverting resources toward litigation and making fewer resources available for advancing strategic goals.

### Intervention

The Chair or any Board member must speak up immediately and demand that staff members be treated with courtesy and respect.

It should be emphasized that the Board must ensure a safe and harassment-free environment and have zero tolerance for abusive behaviors.

As a preventive measure, clarify to Board members that complaints about individual staff members must not be discussed at Board meetings. Instead, such complaints must be referred to the CEO so he or she can address them in private with individual staff members.

PROBLEM

# 82

## RUBBER-STAMPING MANAGEMENT'S RECOMMENDATIONS

In its quest to be efficient, the Board of a nonprofit charity routinely approves CEO and staff recommendations without much questioning. Trust levels are high, and so are apathy, complacency, and acquiescence.

### Potential Damage

The Board may lose its grasp on the organization's business while retaining ultimate accountability. If a flawed decision is implemented, the Board may blame the CEO for proposing it, and the CEO may then blame the Board for not asking the right questions. Regardless of who is found to be guilty, the organization itself is the ultimate victim.

### Intervention

Remind the Board that the CEO, staff, and committees are human and are capable of making mistakes or becoming too passionate about some initiatives. Encourage members to read premeeting material carefully, analyze management's recommendations, and identify areas that need to be questioned. Suggest that they not hesitate to ask questions or even to criticize the quality of staff recommendations, as long as they do not attack their originators.

An example of an unconventional intervention is that of the CEO who planted some obvious mistakes in her report and started her presentation by checking how many Board members discovered them. Her message to the Board was: *"It's very nice that you trust me so much, but your organization needs you to do your homework and be prepared to question my assumptions and conclusions."*

PROBLEM

# 83

## THE DOMINANT CEO

An assertive CEO takes the lead on establishing policies and strategic goals. He expects the Board to rubber-stamp his recommendations without questioning. The problem is exacerbated by the fact that the Board is weak, divided, and somewhat dysfunctional, which gives the CEO even more control.

### Potential Damage

When an overly proactive CEO dominates the Board's agenda, it weakens the Board and renders its governance meaningless. Excessive reliance on the CEO may mean that the Board will be afraid or unable to give the CEO meaningful supervision and oversight. There may be no immediate problem if a CEO is principled, but when one person has so much unchallenged power, his temptation to abuse this power may be too great to resist. If and when a new CEO takes over, the Board may be too weak to assert itself and take charge.

## Intervention

In order to intervene, do not hesitate to challenge and question the CEO or even say no to a proposed initiative. Also, promote more substantial and meaningful engagement of Board members in decision making while explaining the risks of being passive, detached, or acquiescent. Recruit Board members who will not hesitate to ask questions or raise valid concerns. Reassure the CEO that this is not intended to undermine his authority but rather is meant to build Board strength and ensure proper accountability.

PROBLEM

# 84

## GIFTS FROM THE CEO

A CEO concludes her annual report by thanking a few hardworking Board members for their efforts. She then presents those individuals with gifts and tokens of appreciation.

## Potential Damage

Given that the CEO reports to the Board collectively, it is outside her role to reward individual Board members for their efforts. If she is to express any gratitude, it should be directed to the Board as a unit. The CEO's actions in this case can be taken as an attempt to disarm and gain favors with individual members. These actions can make it awkward for those members to criticize and question the CEO or exercise meaningful oversight, supervision, and discipline when needed.

## Intervention

Clarify to the CEO that although recognition of individual Board members for good work is important, the proper party to do it is not the CEO but the Board Chair or possibly a Board committee.

PROBLEM

# 85

## THE STONEWALLING CEO

A smooth-talking CEO has mastered the art of telling the Board what it wants to hear: *"There is nothing to worry about. It was handled this morning,"* or: *"It's not complicated. It will get done this afternoon."* Diligent Board members discover later that nothing got done and that the smooth talk may be a cover for incompetence or negligence. When confronted, the CEO responds with further excuses, and a majority of the Board is content to believe him.

In another setting, the Board is made aware of low staff morale and allegations of verbal abuse and harassment from the CEO or some managers. When questioned about it, the CEO reacts defensively: *"You're micromanaging me now. The Board's role is to set policy, and my role is to implement it. Don't worry. Just let me do my job. Everything is under control."* The Board acquiesces.

### Potential Damage

As concerns persist, trust diminishes. Perceptions of stonewalling and deception grow. It seems like the CEO has built an unchallenged empire, using glib replies and lofty governance theories to avoid scrutiny and thereby maintain substandard performance.

If—as in the second setting described above—staff members are indeed treated inappropriately, they are likely to be distracted from their work and perform at a fraction of their capacity. There is increased risk of staff resignations or even court actions for bullying and harassment by the CEO or some managers.

### Intervention

Given that the Board is ultimately accountable for the organization's performance, it must not allow legitimate concerns to be dismissed by the CEO as micromanagement. If the Board suspects deception or incompetence, it should be less concerned about governance theories and organizational charts and more concerned about risk management. In such cases, the Board must become less detached and trusting and more hands-on. It must demand full disclosure, accountability, honesty, and performance to high standards. If such performance is not forthcoming, the good of the organization may require the Board to replace the CEO.

PROBLEM

# 86

## SANITIZED REPORTS

In an attempt to avoid arguments, a CEO reviews staff reports before distribution to the Board. She removes anything that the Board or some of its vocal members may find offensive or politically unpalatable. In other instances, the CEO tempers strong recommendations because she does not believe the Board can handle community opposition to the proposed initiatives.

### Potential Damage

With honest professional advice being filtered out of reports, the Board is unable to make fully informed decisions or consider viable (though uncomfortable) options. The CEO's assumption that the Board cannot handle bold and necessary initiatives may thereby become a self-fulfilling prophecy. This will likely deprive the community of the smart, thoughtful, and strategic leadership that it deserves.

Staff members whose reports are sanitized are likely to feel insulted and undermined. In addition, if the Board discovers that a report was sanitized and information was deliberately withheld, tensions will likely rise and trust levels will be eroded. The CEO may then suffer consequences for attempting to shield the Board from controversies.

## Intervention

Clarify to the CEO that the Board expects full and honest professional advice, untainted by speculation over how the Board might react to it. In addition, reassure the CEO and the staff that the Board will be grateful for the full disclosure, will never punish a staff member for giving uncomfortable news, and will always focus on the message rather than the messenger.

P R O B L E M

# 87

## PRIVATE BRIEFINGS FROM THE CEO

Fearing an adverse reaction to a contentious report, a CEO invites the most vocal Board member to his office and gives him a private briefing on the matter. The Board finds out about this private conversation in the middle of a meeting when it becomes apparent that one member is more informed than anyone else.

## Potential Damage

Board members who did not receive the private briefing may become angry and suspicious of both the CEO and their colleague. These tensions may distract the Board from the material presented, thereby reducing the Board's ability to make quality decisions in a mature, calm, and measured manner. Perceptions of collusion and preferred treatment may develop and may end up aborting positive and necessary initiatives.

### Intervention

Demand that the CEO and management provide all Board members with the same information at about the same time. The only possible justification for a private briefing is if a Board member does not understand the technical aspects of an issue and everyone else does. Even in such a case, for the sake of transparency, the opportunity of education should be extended to everyone.

PROBLEM

# 88

## WITHHOLDING CRITICISM

While a Board meeting is in progress, two senior staff members joke among themselves about how dysfunctional the Board is. They even place bets on who will be the most disruptive member and how long the meeting will last this time. Sometimes such criticisms are shared via private e-mails, and when they inadvertently become public, a firestorm erupts.

### Potential Damage

Staff members who voice criticism of the Board in the background undermine the Board and deprive it of the feedback it needs to become effective. This situation ultimately compromises the leadership that the Board and the professional staff must jointly provide to the community. If Board members find out about such unexpressed feedback, they will be justifiably angry.

### Intervention

Facilitate regular exchanges of feedback between the Board and management, along the lines of: *"Here is what you can do to help us serve the organization,"* and *"Here is what you sometimes do that reduces our ability to deliver optimal results."* Such discussions should occur frequently, so individuals will talk *to* one another rather than talk *about* one another.

As a matter of caution, staff members should treat all their comments, whether off or on the record, as public record: The walls have ears. One never knows when a personal e-mail is inadvertently sent or forwarded to unintended recipients or when a comment made in private is picked up by a microphone or overheard by a third party or a media reporter. The safest assumption to make is that all comments could be discussed on the six o'clock news.

PROBLEM

# 89

## OVERUSE OR UNDERUSE OF CONSULTANTS

A Board relies extensively on lawyers, management consultants, and other advisers. It hesitates to make tough decisions unless all grounds are fully covered by consultants. In some instances, a Board looks for specific answers, and when it gets contradictory answers from one expert, it retains another. In other cases, a Board becomes dependent on an external meeting Chair, despite her offers to teach facilitation skills to willing Board officers.

On the opposite extreme is the Board that, in an attempt to save money or with the notion of *"We know all there is to know,"* refuses to hire a much needed expert to address a complex issue.

### Potential Damage

Although well-targeted expert advice can provide essential knowledge, excessive dependence on experts can erode the Board's backbone and confidence. It can become an avoidance mechanism and may delay tough decisions that must be made. It can make a Board appear tentative, weak, and indecisive.

Conversely, a Board that refuses to retain advisers whose expertise is critical to good decision making will be pooling its ignorance and may be making decisions that it will regret. By its stinginess, the Board will save a little money now, but it could lose much more later on.

## Intervention

Use consultants smartly. Do not look for engineering advice from a lawyer or legal advice from an architect. Establish the questions that need to be answered and disclose all relevant data to the consultant. It may be prudent to have the consultant interview key individuals within the organization to help the consultant understand the full scope of the issues before rendering the advice. It is also wise to invest in a written report covering the consultant's findings.

If the consultant presents the advice and then answers questions at a Board meeting, it may work well in some cases to ask him or her to leave at some point, to ensure a free-flowing Board discussion without the potentially stifling effect of the consultant's presence.

In general, it is best to retain consultants who share their knowledge freely and are not preoccupied by trying to protect it. A consultant's search for more business should be secondary to the goal of providing quality advice and building client knowledge and strength.

If your Board is reluctant to invest in essential expert advice, you may need to remind it of the phrase *"pay a little bit now, or you may pay a lot more later on."* Prudent investment in expert advice is likely to add depth to discussions, boost the quality of any consensus, and reduce the likelihood of costly mistakes.

# 90

# INTERFERING WITH AN ADVISER

A Board member who happens to be a lawyer or an accountant has many ideas on how the hired legal counsel or auditor should do his job. In another scenario, the Board Chair hires an impartial facilitator to lead a contentious meeting, then tells her what facilitation techniques she should use and what outcomes and consensus she should lead to.

## Potential Damage

Interference by a client may distract an external adviser or facilitator, especially when refusal to follow a client's order may mean the loss of a paying assignment. Some advisers may be so afraid of offending their bullying client that they are deterred from delivering necessary but unpopular advice, thereby shortchanging the organization. Similarly, an external facilitator will lose her credibility as a trusted and impartial professional if she leads a contentious meeting and works to achieve a predetermined outcome as desired by the Board Chair.

## Intervention

Abandon the practice of second-guessing professional advisers or facilitators or telling them how to do their jobs and what advice to give or not give. As the saying goes, *"If you hire a chef, stay out of the kitchen."* A Board member who becomes aware that the Chair or another person is interfering with the work of an adviser should raise the concern with the individual or with the Board.

Hired professionals should have the strength and integrity to demand the leeway they need to perform to their best. If not given such leeway, they should not hesitate to abandon the assignment and the monetary compensation that comes with it.

## PROBLEM
# 91
## THE TIMID MINUTE TAKER

A minute taker is not sure about the Board's consensus or the wording of a motion and is afraid to ask for clarification. On some occasions, she has significant information that the Board could benefit from but does not share it since she is too timid to speak up.

### Potential Damage

Without a clearly worded motion recorded in the minutes, there will be uncertainty about what the Board's decision was, which may generate confusion and risks for the organization. It may also cause arguments about the wording of the motion at the next meeting, possibly after the unclear decision was implemented.

If the minute taker has essential knowledge that no one else present at the meeting has and she does not share it, flawed decisions may be made. If Board members discover later that the minute taker could have helped them prevent a bad decision or make a better one, they would be justifiably angry and disappointed.

### Intervention

Treat the minute taker as a partner in the decision-making process, make it acceptable for her to speak up, and establish the protocol for her to do so in a public meeting. It may be by raising a hand, passing a note to the Chair, or another method. Establish a balance whereby the Board can govern and make decisions while benefitting from the staff's knowledge.

To prevent a vote on an unclear motion, the practice should be for the minute taker to ask that the motion be clarified, or she may read it aloud and request confirmation of the exact wording.

# CHAPTER TEN

# FLAWED
# INTERACTIONS WITH
# THE COMMUNITY

·

The community is the set of individuals and groups that the Board is mandated to serve. Many Boards are elected periodically by the community and are collectively accountable to the community as a whole. To operate effectively, a Board must treat its community as a partner in decision making. Being disconnected from the community can create problems ranging from skepticism, cynicism, and mistrust to vociferous opposition, civil disobedience, and organized efforts to oust the Board.

This chapter discusses flawed interactions between the Board and the community. Although several examples in this chapter are from governmental Boards, similar dynamics can occur during shareholder meetings, general meetings of nonprofit organizations, and other settings.

PROBLEM

# 92

## ENTRENCHMENT AND DEFENSIVENESS

Faced with community opposition to a contentious initiative, a Community Board spends much time and effort defending its decisions and dismissing criticism. The louder the opposition gets, the more entrenched the Board becomes. The Board is especially defensive in reacting to special interest groups and resents the tactics these groups use to advance their agendas. The Board routinely hires public relations experts and media trainers to help its spokespersons sell the Board's message.

### Potential Damage

Small disputes can escalate into costly controversies that may breed adversarial actions or even lawsuits, thereby wasting resources, discrediting the Board, and distracting it from its mandate. Special interest groups may outmaneuver the Board on the public relations front.

### Intervention

Make proactive efforts to listen and learn about community concerns. Find out which concerns are valid, make necessary changes to decisions, and keep the community informed. It may also be wise to retain a trusted third party to plan and facilitate a community consultation program. This should be done with the clear understanding with the community that its input will be advisory and nonbinding, as the Board cannot abrogate its legislated mandate to govern.

The Board should not fault special interest groups for being determined and having their own agendas, but the Board should ensure that it too has its own agenda. A proactive Board would develop a long-term (macro) agenda at the start of its term of office, obtain professional input on it from management and outside experts, and then involve the community in dialogue about it. Once this process is completed, all proposed initiatives (including those requested by community groups) would receive priority only if they fit well with the Board's macro agenda.

PROBLEM

# 93

## CAPITULATION TO POLITICAL PRESSURE

A prominent citizen advocates on behalf of a special interest group to her Municipal Council. She puts forth an impassioned plea for financial support. She threatens election-time consequences for council members if her request is denied. Her group is well represented in the public seating area. The citizen's presentation compels a council member to immediately move that the funding be granted, as it seems like a politically wise thing to do. It is awkward for other members to oppose the proposal and for senior staff to question it in front of such an eloquent presenter from the community. The financial support is granted with no real scrutiny.

### Potential Damage

The decision is driven by emotion and political pressure, rather than by a professional and objective approach backed by expert analysis. The council responds to and accommodates the eloquent presenter and the group of citizens in front of it, possibly at the expense of the community as a whole. The fact that management had no time to study this impulsively made motion means that the decision will likely create financial and operational challenges. In addition, other interest groups will likely follow this precedent and use coercion and manipulation to advance their goals.

### Intervention

As awkward as it may be, the Council should revisit this impulsive decision at a subsequent meeting, this time with the benefit of professional analysis. To prevent impulsive decisions in the future, slow the process down. Delay decisions on impromptu motions until a subsequent meeting, request professional advice, and avoid capitulating to political bullying by small but influential community groups.

PROBLEM

# 94

## BEHIND CLOSED DOORS

A local public Board has many closed meetings, simply because the agenda items discussed might be too embarrassing or inconvenient to discuss in a public setting.

### Potential Damage

Transparency and accountability are damaged, as is the Board's credibility. With so many issues being dealt with in secret, rumors spread fast and poison the air. Public trust is eroded, and the validity of Board decisions may be challenged, possibly in court, on the grounds that they should have been made in open sessions. Time and money may thereby be diverted toward damage control, making fewer resources available for strategic priorities.

### Intervention

Teach your Board to balance the need for transparency with the need for risk management. Ensure that most decisions are made in public and that no issue is placed on a closed meeting agenda without valid reasons. Such reasons are likely to be documented in your applicable legislation, bylaws, or policies. They usually include protecting the privacy of third parties and protecting the organization's interests. Typical closed meeting topics include hiring or firing decisions, legal advice on sensitive matters, labor negotiations or other contracts, the sale or acquisition of land, and choosing a person to receive an award.

Avoid scheduling open meeting items and closed meeting items on the same agenda, since this can be frustrating for observers (who must leave when the Board goes into a closed session without knowing when to return) and confusing for the minute taker (for whom it is a challenge to keep separate minutes for open and closed sessions). Instead, schedule two separate meetings, one open and one closed, and hold them one after the other, with separate minutes kept for each. Minutes of a closed meeting should be kept confidential and should include only the topics and the decisions made, but no attempt should be made to summarize the discussion.

If an issue is on a closed meeting agenda without a valid reason, the Board should transfer it to the next open meeting agenda. Conversely, if a closed meeting issue is mistakenly placed on an open meeting agenda, it should be transferred to the next closed meeting agenda.

PROBLEM
# 95
## BREACHES OF CONFIDENTIALITY

A Board member leaks information from a closed meeting to his spouse, family, the public, or the media.

### Potential Damage

Breaches of confidentiality are damaging in two ways. First, placing sensitive information in the public domain can lead to invasions of the privacy of third parties or can expose the organization to risk. The second casualty of leaks is the trust among Board members. In subsequent closed meetings, members may not speak frankly and openly, for fear that their words will appear in the newspapers or on the evening news. Full and spontaneous participation is thereby curtailed and flawed decisions become more likely.

## Intervention

Schedule a Board discussion about breaches of confidentiality and highlight the damage they inflict. It is best to do this at Board orientation time. Explain that if members believe an item does not belong on a closed meeting agenda, they should raise their concerns so the Board can address them collectively. If, after consideration of such concerns, the Board decides to keep the item on the closed meeting agenda, everyone (including dissenters) must respect this decision, keep the proceedings confidential, and avoid any leaks.

If, after warnings, it can be proved that a member continued to leak information from closed meetings, you may need to pursue disciplinary measures under your legislation or bylaws.

PROBLEM
# 96
## BOARD ACTING AS A COMPLAINT DEPARTMENT

In its efforts to be popular with citizens, a Municipal Council discusses all letters addressed to the mayor and the council as the first item in its meetings. In addition, council members who receive complaints from citizens privately between meetings respond to them by promising: *"I'll make it go away for you at the next council meeting,"* instead of directing the complaints to staff for assessment.

## Potential Damage

Citizens who have the time and skill to write letters receive a great deal of airtime at the beginning of council meetings. Such actions waste time and distract the council from concentrating on its mandate and mission and the needs of the community as a whole. By the time larger issues that affect the broader community are reached, council members may be tired and saturated, and their ability to learn from discussions and make informed decisions with fresh minds is bound to be reduced.

Promises made by council members to citizens privately prior to meetings make it awkward for members to keep an open mind during meetings. Having made such promises, their ability to act objectively and serve the interests of the community as a whole is severely impaired.

## Intervention

The council should muster its collective courage and establish a policy to delegate complaints by individual citizens to the staff, except when they point to larger issues that affect the entire community. Meetings should be structured and timed to keep council members fresh and alert, especially when dealing with significant issues that affect the community as a whole. Members who receive complaints from the public between meetings should usually refer them to staff. They must resist the temptation to give premeeting promises on how they will vote on issues.

# 97

# NO BOUNDARIES BETWEEN THE
# BOARD AND THE COMMUNITY

While a Board meeting is in progress, a prominent community member walks in to the public seating area. The Board Chair says spontaneously: *"Come join us,"* and the citizen is seated at the Board table. Elsewhere, the Municipal Council of a small community runs meetings very informally, and citizens speak whenever they want to. In the middle of a meeting, a citizen shouts: *"Point of order. You're doing this all wrong."*

## Potential Damage

With no boundaries between the Board and the citizens in attendance, the Board's ability to govern and provide leadership to the full community is diminished. This is especially problematic when the Board needs to make decisions that the citizens in attendance object to. The Board's capacity to say no to a persistent community group is nonexistent if the group's representatives can speak whenever they want and effectively function as unelected Board members. The fact that non-Board members do not vote does not diminish their influence and ability to deprive the remainder of the community (which is not in attendance) of the Board's leadership.

## Intervention

Establish, communicate, and enforce the rule that observers must be seated away from the Board table and that they may participate only when invited to do so by the Board and only under the Board's rules. Prepare a welcome sheet for observers, explaining how meetings are run, when observers can provide input, and for how long. Write a script for the Chair to welcome the public, explain the agenda, and highlight the main rules for the meeting.

If observers speak outside the established protocol, the Chair should intervene. If the Chair does not intervene, any other Board member may raise the appropriate point of order: *"Point of order. With all due respect, the time for citizens to speak has passed, and discussion should now be within the Board."*

PROBLEM

# 98
## CHEERING, CLAPPING, HECKLING, AND HARASSMENT

A public hearing is called to receive input from community groups about a contentious rezoning bylaw, and some factions are well represented. People applaud and cheer speakers with whom they agree and heckle speakers with whom they disagree.

### Potential Damage

The meeting environment becomes intimidating, and many people find it unsafe to participate, especially if they hold minority views. The emotional bias makes it unlikely that civil, objective, and rational debates will occur, which is bound to diminish the usefulness of public input. The intense pressure may intimidate the Board and cause it to abandon positive and necessary initiatives (which may disenfranchise the community as a whole). Loud and aggressive groups, who represent only a fraction of the community, may in effect become the decision makers who determine public policy.

There is yet another risk to consider: Citizens who feel unsafe speaking may be so distraught that they may launch court action against the organization, alleging that they were subjected to bullying and harassment, that it was unsafe for them to speak, and that the Board did nothing about it. The validity of some Board decisions may be challenged on this basis.

### Intervention

Write the public hearing notice and the Chair's opening remarks to acknowledge the contentious nature of the issues at hand. Then outline the rules that the public will be required to follow to ensure a civil, orderly, and productive debate. Ask everyone to help make it safe for people to offer their observations, regardless of their views. Emphasize that cheering, clapping, heckling, and other disruptive behaviors will not be tolerated.

If cheering, clapping, or heckling do occur, stop the person who is speaking and call for order. If the audience does not cooperate, call a break. After the break, remind the audience of the rules and warn them that if the conduct does not improve, there will be no option but to adjourn the meeting. Point out that—if the meeting is indeed adjourned—those who are waiting to speak will be disenfranchised. If it is legally permissible, an alternative backup plan may be to ask the different factions to identify their spokespersons and then hear from them in private, instead of hearing from all of them together in one large meeting.

PROBLEM

# 99

## MISGUIDED FOCUS ON THE CUSTOMER

A corporate Board, acting on management's advice, continues to support the production and marketing of goods that have been proved to be harmful to people and the environment. The Board acts on the premise that *"as long as our customers demand these products and are prepared to pay for them, we will continue to make them available."*

In another setting, a public Board responds to a poll showing that a majority of citizens favor a certain initiative. Some Board members object to it and cite reports that indicate unacceptable long-term costs. But most Board members seem to want to govern by the polls, especially when an election is looming. The prevailing notion is *"the customer is always right."*

## Potential Damage

The long-term good of the community is compromised when popularity and polling numbers are placed ahead of professional judgment and long-range thinking. Communities of the future, made up of the children and grandchildren of today's citizens, will resent the low-grade leadership that did not have the strength to make unpopular yet visionary decisions.

## Intervention

Make Board members aware that their real customer may not be the community of today but the organization as a whole and its long-term future. Encourage the Board to proactively set the direction and values for the organization, rather than just follow popular opinions. It may also be necessary to educate citizens about the need to make some inconvenient choices today so the community and its environment are kept sustainable for future generations.

P R O B L E M

# 100

## UNPROFESSIONAL APPEARANCE AT PUBLIC MEETINGS

Some members of a public Board wear jeans, shorts, gym clothes, or other casual attire to public meetings. During meetings, they lean back or rock in their chairs or stare blankly at the ceiling or their computer screens. Sometimes they frown, wink, smile, or nod enthusiastically when citizens make presentations. When they are frustrated, they roll their eyes or throw their pens on the table. Some direct their comments to the TV cameras or their supporters who are seated in the public gallery. Some eat or chew gum while in front of the public. When criticized for these behaviors, the Board members become defensive and pledge that they will always act as *one of the people* and will never place themselves in a separate class.

## Potential Damage

The Board appears unprofessional. Even if the members make good decisions, their casual appearances may lower the Board's credibility and make it look less than trustworthy when dealing with significant decisions and large budgets. Appearances can definitely send messages:

- Wearing jeans or casual attire or eating or chewing gum may not convey the image of well-focused leaders whom people will instinctively trust. Casual attire may also cast doubt on a member's ability to make unpopular decisions when confronted by loud public opposition.

- Leaning back or rocking back and forth in a chair may convey a message of being arrogant, laid back, disengaged, and apathetic.

- Staring blankly at the ceiling or the computer screen may convey the impression of daydreaming or being disinterested in what is being said at the meeting.

- Rolling eyes or throwing pens on the table displays impatience and immaturity. They are not the behaviors of measured, responsible, thoughtful, and trustworthy decision makers.

- Winking or exchanging looks with others gives the impression of collusion, backroom dealing, disrespect, and hidden agendas.

- Smiling or nodding enthusiastically when a citizen speaks sends a message of approval. This can be seen to indicate that the Board member has made up his or her mind and is not genuinely open to other views. Frowning when a citizen speaks conveys a dismissive attitude and is similarly problematic. Keeping a poker face is best.

- Directing comments at TV cameras or the public gallery (instead of addressing the Board) may convey the impression of grandstanding and egotism.

## Intervention

At Board orientation, explain that professional appearances enhance, elevate, and show respect for the position that elected members occupy. Emphasize that an elevated stature for elected officials is essential for effective trusteeship and decision making.

Show how a sloppy and unprofessional appearance can diminish trust in the Board. Emphasize the principle that justice must not only be done but must also be seen to be done. With this in mind, Board members must listen and appear to be listening with open minds. They must not appear to be impatient or dismissive, nor should they appear to be supportive of certain views, especially when issues are contentious or when the Board members act in a quasi-judicial capacity.

Stress that although some public input is driven by emotion, ignorance, and self-interest, it is still incumbent on Board members to search for valid and useful input, even when it appears to be buried in predictable or useless data or when a speaker's logic seems very flawed.

Consider taping some meetings and showing the footage to the Board as feedback. Let Board members answer this question for themselves: *"Do I act and appear like someone who can be trusted with the community's assets and future?"*

## PROBLEM
# 101

# SPEECHES DISGUISED AS QUESTIONS

After a citizen's presentation, a Board member asks questions in a hostile or condescending tone. Another Board member asks leading questions to guide the citizen toward making a certain point. Yet another Board member prefaces a question with a long speech.

## Potential Damage

Although these statements are framed as questions, they really are speeches and advocacy statements. They effectively engage citizens in debate with elected officials, and this debate is inherently unfair because Board members vote and citizens don't. They may also convey a message of bias in favor of or against a certain viewpoint. They seriously compromise the principle that Board members must listen to citizens' presentations with open minds and a genuine desire to learn.

## Intervention

Advise members that when asking questions of citizens, they must make them purely clarifying and brief questions, without engaging the citizens in debate and without explicitly or implicitly expressing approval or disapproval of a certain point of view. If Board members violate this rule, the Chair or another Board member should raise a point of order and demand that speeches be avoided and that only clarifying questions be permitted.

# APPENDIX A

# BOARD EFFECTIVENESS AUDIT

This appendix provides a series of questions that can assist you in auditing your foundation for Board decision making. These lists are a compilation of key questions raised throughout this book. Use them to assess your Board's capacity for effective and efficient decision making and its immunity to dysfunctions. See Appendix B for more detailed Board evaluation tools.

### 1. Mission, Vision, and Strategy

- Is your mission compelling and relevant to current realities? Are people passionate about it?

- Does the Board have a clear vision of an ideal and perfect organization?

- Does the Board have a strategy to fulfill its mission and make its vision a reality?

- Is the strategy divided into manageable components that can be scheduled and implemented?

- Are the mission, vision, and strategy evident in how the organization is governed and managed?

See Chapter One for related Boardroom problems.

### 2. Decision-Making Structures

- Is the Board sufficiently large to be representative of its constituents?

- Is the Board sufficiently small to allow flexible and efficient decision making?

- Are there mechanisms to hold the Board accountable to its community?

- Are decision-making powers logically allocated between the Board and management?

- Are the rules on voting and quorum clear and logical?

See Chapter Two for related Boardroom problems.

### 3. Organizational Culture

- Are there principles and core values that serve as the organization's conscience?

- Do people within the organization demand excellence of themselves and others?

- Is there an appropriate balance between trust and healthy skepticism?

- Is there tolerance of dissent and an ability to benefit from disagreements?

- Does a culture of service and community override the culture of entitlement?

See Chapter Three for related Boardroom problems.

## 4. The Board as a Whole

■ Is the Board working as a team while benefiting from independent thinking?

■ Is the Board providing high-level stewardship without being distracted by minutiae?

■ Does the Board ask tough questions and demand excellence and accountability from management?

■ Does the Board build strong relationships with its community and stakeholders?

■ Does the Board regularly evaluate itself and its meetings? (See Appendix B.)

See Chapters Four and Seven for related Boardroom problems.

## 5. Individual Board Members

■ Are Board members selected based on knowledge, skill, attitude, and commitment levels?

■ Is there an appropriate mix on the Board (seasoned versus new, age, gender, and so on)?

■ Do members receive meaningful orientation, mentoring, continuing education, and skill building?

■ Are members engaged in Board decision making? Do they excel and perform follow-up duties?

■ Is member performance monitored against set criteria? Do members receive feedback regularly?

See Chapter Five for related Boardroom problems.

## 6. The Board Chair

■ Does the Chair act as a role model, mentor, team builder, and consensus builder?

- Does the Chair balance the needs for efficiency, inclusiveness, and effective decision making?

- Does the Chair have the backbone to say no when needed, firmly but graciously?

- Does the Chair have the necessary articulation, listening, and leadership skills?

- Does the Chair train successors and build the Board's leadership base?

See Chapter Six for related Boardroom problems.

### 7. Committees

- Do committees have clear and meaningful mandates and schedules?

- Are committee members selected on merit? Are they oriented for their work?

- Do committees deliver substantial results? Are they held accountable?

- Do committees operate within their powers (which are advisory, unless specified otherwise)?

- Are committees disbanded when they are no longer needed?

### 8. The CEO and Management

- Is the CEO accountable, open, nondefensive, and accessible to the Board?

- Does the CEO regularly share feedback with and take feedback from the Board?

- Does the CEO provide high-quality professional advice in a timely manner?

- Does the CEO bring out the best in the management and staff teams?

- Does the CEO create a safe and harassment-free work environment?

See Chapter Nine for related Boardroom problems.

### 9. The Community and Stakeholders

- Does the community elect principled leaders and demand excellence from them?

- Is the community engaged and interested in Board decision making?

- Does the community provide input and advice to the Board?

- Does the community know and abide by the rules and laws that govern the organization?

- Does the community understand and support the focus on long-term and holistic outcomes?

See Chapter Ten for related Boardroom problems.

### 10. Rules of Interaction

- Do Board and committee members place collective interests ahead of narrow interests?

- Are there efforts to learn from dissenting views and achieve broad consensus?

- If unanimity is not possible, do dissenting members accept collective decisions?

- Are members aware of and do they abide by conflict of interest guidelines?

- Do members keep confidentiality? Do they know the risks of breaches of confidentiality?

See Chapters Three and Four for related Boardroom problems.

### 11. Meetings

- Are meeting agendas linked to the organization's mission, vision, and strategy?

- Are agenda items and decision-making options researched in advance of meetings?

- Do meetings achieve quality outcomes inclusively and at a comfortable pace?

- Do members listen with open minds, learn from debates, and make knowledge-based decisions?

- Are rules of order used appropriately to facilitate progress and ensure equality and fairness?

See Chapter Eight for related Boardroom problems.

### 12. Feedback and Dispute Resolution

- Is feedback shared regularly at all levels?

- Is corrective feedback balanced by kudos and regular expressions of appreciation?

- Are there timely and decisive interventions to address counterproductive behaviors?

- Are there mechanisms to prevent, detect, and resolve disputes?

- Are disciplinary measures in place? Is there readiness to apply them when needed?

See Appendix B for Board evaluation tools.

# APPENDIX B

# BOARD EVALUATION TOOLS

Here are ten steps to achieve excellence on your Board:

1. Recruit effective Board members.

2. Give Board members the knowledge and skills they need to optimize their performance. Provide refreshers and continuing education as new issues emerge.

3. Hold an annual orientation for the Board as a whole, and insist that all members—new and experienced—attend.

4. Quickly engage new Board members in meaningful work, and keep them involved.

5. Regularly recognize the contributions of Board members, both privately and publicly.

6. Make meetings relevant and interactive, and link them to the Board's strategic plan.

7. Arrange to have every Board meeting evaluated.

8. Arrange for self-evaluation or peer evaluation of Board members.

9. Regularly evaluate the Board's relationship with the CEO and management.

10. Regularly evaluate the Board's relationship with its community and stakeholders.

As the above ten steps indicate, feedback and evaluation are critical to the Board's continued effectiveness. This appendix discusses feedback and evaluation and covers the following topics:

1. General Tips for Giving Feedback

2. General Tips for Taking Feedback

3. Evaluating a Board Member

4. Evaluating a Board Chair

5. Evaluating a Board Collectively

6. Evaluating a Meeting

7. Evaluating a CEO

8. Evaluating a Community

Each of the evaluation forms in the last six sections (covering "Evaluating a Board Member" through "Evaluating a Community") has ten rows. Each row represents one evaluation category and earns a score of up to 10 points. The grand total score for the ten evaluation categories will be between 0 and 100, fitting within the following ranges:

| Total Score | Description | What's Needed to Improve |
|---|---|---|
| 91 to 100 | Excellent | You are doing exceptionally well. Still, do not take things for granted. Maintain strength by monitoring, sharing feedback, and setting new goals. |

| Total Score | Description | What's Needed to Improve |
|---|---|---|
| 71 to 90 | Effective | You are doing well, but there is still work to be done to achieve excellence. |
| 51 to 70 | Mediocre | The work gets done, yet the results are not inspiring. |
| 0 to 50 | Dysfunctional | Serious change is needed, but progress is within reach. Talk about the scores and discuss how to improve performance. |

# 1. GENERAL TIPS FOR GIVING FEEDBACK

Feedback is the lifeblood of a well-functioning organization. Its abundant presence means that problems can be detected and addressed in a timely manner and that the damage they inflict can be minimized. The absence of feedback breeds dysfunctions.

Despite the benefits of feedback, many people dread it. Therefore, as the giver of feedback, you need to make it easy for others to receive it and learn from it. Consider these tips:

- Give feedback regularly. Don't wait until the problem is acute or the situation is unbearable. By then, it may be too difficult to repair the damage.

- Give the feedback only after establishing that the other party is ready to hear you: *"I have some feedback for you. When would be a convenient time to discuss it?"*

- Deliver the feedback with the premise that the recipient is capable of reasonable behavior, even if past events have given you reasons to doubt this assumption. You may discover that the person is not doing things maliciously and is unaware of the damage caused by certain behaviors.

- Connect the discussion to overriding principles that no one will question. Show how problematic behaviors diminish the Board's capacity to serve the community that everyone, including the recipient of the feedback, cares about.

- Make the feedback interactive and consultative, and avoid lecturing. Punctuate the feedback by asking questions, such as: *"Can you see why that is a problem for us?"* or: *"How does this fit with you?"* Be prepared to learn from the interaction.

- Make the feedback clear, specific, and objective. Be hard on issues but soft on the person. Focus on behaviors, not emotions or personalities. Be honest and direct.

- Make the feedback balanced. State positive observations in the form of praise and suggested changes in the form of recommendations.

- Avoid long preambles or apologies, which dilute and weaken the feedback and make it difficult for the listener to figure out what you are trying to say.

- Avoid a harsh, accusatory, or condescending tone. Whenever possible, replace negative phrases with affirmative ones. For example, replace *"Here are the things you do wrong"* with *"Here is what you could do to help us achieve better results."*

- In complex situations, you may want to start by jointly defining the problem. Ask for the other party's understanding of the problem, and then share yours. This approach will achieve two goals: It may teach you things you did not know about the situation, and it will likely build collaboration and mutual respect. Only after exploring the problem should you start to identify solutions. If you start with solutions too quickly, you may encounter resistance or find yourself solving the wrong problem.

- Lead to an agreement on what changes need to occur, establish deadlines for implementing them, and follow up at designated times. It may be necessary to put the agreement in writing to ensure that promises can be followed up on.

## 2. GENERAL TIPS FOR TAKING FEEDBACK

Feedback from others can help you correct annoying behaviors and improve your performance. Given that it is very difficult or even frightening for many people to give feedback, you must make it easy for them to share it with you. Here are a few tips:

- Treat feedback as a gift. Welcome a complaint with the same enthusiasm that you would greet a compliment. Go as far as rewarding or publicly recognizing those who shared feedback and made a difference by doing so.

- Solicit feedback proactively and create opportunities for others to give it to you. For example, at the end of a meeting, say: *"Does anyone have any feedback on how the meeting went? I promise I will not be offended. I would also welcome your feedback after the meeting if you need time to think about it."*

- When someone gives you feedback, show genuine interest in it. Ask open-ended questions to learn from the feedback and help the other person clarify what he is saying: *"Tell me more. What do you mean when you say {fill in the blank}?"* Alternatively, you could say: *"I think I'm missing something here: {fill in the blank}. Can you clarify it for me?"*

- Don't be distracted if the tone of the feedback is harsh or aggressive. Just pay attention to the content. Eventually, the individual may calm down, but if you try to control her delivery too quickly, you may end up aggravating or stifling her.

- Having heard the feedback, confirm what you learned and ask if you captured everything correctly: *"Let me check if I understand what you're saying: {fill in the blank}. Is there anything I missed?"* Listen openly to the response and learn from it. Then thank the individual for sharing the feedback.

- Follow up and take corrective action if needed. If you are not able to implement a suggestion, let the giver of the feedback know why; otherwise, the individual may become cynical and withhold the gift of feedback from you in the future.

■ Do not hesitate to apologize if warranted. No one is perfect. Your apology will make it clear that you are human and did not act with malice.

■ Avoid taking feedback as a personal attack. Also avoid interrupting the presenter or instinctively denying the validity of the feedback with *"yes, but"* responses.

■ Resist the temptation to pretend to appreciate the feedback but then trivialize it by thinking: *"This is just one person. Everyone else is telling me what a great job I'm doing."* Remember: For every person who takes the time to complain, there may be ten others who have the same observation but don't bother to share it.

■ If the feedback you receive is positive, be gracious and appreciative. Do not dismiss it by saying: *"You're too kind. I don't deserve this compliment."* The latter statement can come across as dismissive and insulting to the feedback giver. Just say: *"Thank you very much. It is nice to have my work appreciated."*

## 3. EVALUATING A BOARD MEMBER

To ensure continued effectiveness, it is also important to monitor and evaluate the performance of Board members and provide them with feedback. Consider these options:

■ *Self-Evaluation:* Include self-evaluation forms in meeting packages. Remind Board members to complete their forms before leaving the meeting.

■ *Peer Evaluation:* Arrange for feedback on strengths and weaknesses to be given to each member by an assigned colleague or mentor or, alternatively, by the Board Chair.

This section includes two evaluation forms for Board members. The first form is general and can be used periodically, such as during an annual Board retreat. The second form is specific to meetings. It can be given to members at each Board meeting so they can evaluate their own performance just before the meeting is adjourned.

## General Evaluation for a Board Member

| | Ineffective Board Member<br>0 means *as bad as it gets* | Effective Board Member<br>10 means *as good as it gets* | Score<br>0 to 10 |
|---|---|---|---|
| 1 | Joins the Board mainly to socialize; gain business contacts; advance visibility, stature, and influence; or earn an honorarium. | Joins the Board altruistically to help advance its mandate and serve the community. | |
| 2 | Brings a low commitment level. Misses meetings, declines to take on any work, and always has excuses for nonperformance. | Is reliable and conscientious. Prepares fully for meetings, attends them regularly, takes on assignments, and always delivers quality results. | |
| 3 | Tolerates mediocrity, substandard decisions, and/or flawed processes. Has limited interest in innovation and creativity. | Demands excellence of self and of others. Introduces freshness, creativity, and innovation. | |
| 4 | Has a need to be popular with others and does not raise valid concerns about potentially risky decisions. Does not complain about dysfunctions, except after a meeting. | Is prepared to raise tough questions, even if they slow things down, in order to help reduce risk. Does not hesitate to complain about meeting problems in a timely fashion. | |

## General Evaluation for a Board Member (continued)

| | Ineffective Board Member<br>**0 means *as bad as it gets*** | Effective Board Member<br>**10 means *as good as it gets*** | Score<br>**0 to 10** |
|---|---|---|---|
| 5 | Is a single-issue advocate. Joins the Board primarily to promote a narrow interest. Has a closed mind and unchangeable views and is not interested in learning from others. | Places broad interests ahead of narrow ones. Keeps an open mind and has a natural curiosity. Is eager to learn from others and thereby make informed and balanced decisions. | |
| 6 | Is unprincipled. Creates alliances and makes backroom deals to manipulate decisions. Finds the right words to promote the wrong goals. Will do anything to get reelected. | Is honest, principled, selfless, and trustworthy. Acts with integrity. Promotes and embodies core principles and values. Sees reelection as much less important than doing the right things. | |
| 7 | Is egotistical and functions as a lone operator. Treats others with disrespect. Is irritable and uptight. Takes questions as personal attacks. Is quick to dismiss new ideas. | Is humble and ego-free and functions as a team player. Treats others as valued colleagues and partners. Is mature, calm, patient, lighthearted, and thick-skinned. | |
| 8 | Undermines and attacks Board decisions publicly after they are made. Presents personal views as Board positions. | Accepts Board decisions and assists in implementing them. Correctly represents the Board when requested to do so. | |
| 9 | Abuses powers for personal gain. Denies the existence of blatant conflicts of interest. | Adheres to the Board's code of ethics. Discloses conflicts of interest in a timely manner. | |

## General Evaluation for a Board Member (continued)

|    | Ineffective Board Member<br>0 means *as bad as it gets* | Effective Board Member<br>10 means *as good as it gets* | Score<br>0 to 10 |
|----|------------------------------------|----------------------------------|---------|
| 10 | Leaks confidential information from closed meetings, thereby damaging trust and exposing the organization to risk. | Keeps Board confidentiality. Questions the inclusion of items on a closed meeting agenda without valid reasons for it. | |
|    | **GRAND TOTAL** | Add the numbers in the righthand column. (Minimum = 0. Maximum = 100.) | |

## Postmeeting Evaluation for a Board Member

|   | Question | Score<br>0 to 10 |
|---|----------|---------|
| 1 | Did I fully complete my premeeting follow-up duties and tasks? Did I do so with excellence? | |
| 2 | Did I fully review the meeting package? Did I make sufficient efforts to upgrade my knowledge and understanding of the issues on the agenda? | |
| 3 | Did I arrive on time? Was I there for the entire meeting, in body and in spirit? Did I turn off my cell phone? Did I avoid any distractions and give my full attention to the discussions? | |
| 4 | Did I share my ideas when needed? Did I not hesitate to raise necessary questions and valid concerns, even when they might have been unpopular with some members or slowed things down? | |
| 5 | Was I prepared to raise concerns about breaches of meeting protocols when the Chair or others did not intervene? | |

## Postmeeting Evaluation for a Board Member (continued)

| | Question | Score 0 to 10 |
|---|---|---|
| 6 | Did I make room for others to contribute? Did I listen with an open mind? Did I learn from my colleagues and integrate their ideas into my thought process? | |
| 7 | Was I guided by the organization's mission, vision, and strategic plan throughout the meeting? | |
| 8 | Did I always place the interests of the organization and its stakeholders ahead of personal interests or constituency interests? | |
| 9 | Did I act objectively and maturely and in a trustworthy manner? Did I avoid anger or defensiveness? Did I refuse to allow a negative climate to hamper my participation? | |
| 10 | Did I follow the rules of debate and decorum? Did I keep my comments brief and to the point? Did I focus on issues, and did I avoid engaging in personal attacks? | |
| | **GRAND TOTAL** (Minimum = 0. Maximum = 100.) | |

# 4. EVALUATING A BOARD CHAIR

The following table can be used to evaluate your Board Chair.

| | Ineffective Board Chair 0 means *as bad as it gets* | Effective Board Chair 10 means *as good as it gets* | Score 0 to 10 |
|---|---|---|---|
| 1 | Takes the job for the power or financial benefits. Is intoxicated by the visibility with the media and the public. Refuses to share the spotlight with others. | Takes the job in order to serve and make a difference. Is selfless and committed to the organization's mission and the community. | |

## Evaluating a Board Chair (continued)

| | Ineffective Board Chair<br>0 means *as bad as it gets* | Effective Board Chair<br>10 means *as good as it gets* | Score<br>0 to 10 |
|---|---|---|---|
| 2 | Is used to making unilateral decisions and giving orders to others. Biases debates in favor of certain outcomes. Uses threats and bullying. | Leads the Board in consensus building and making collective decisions. Engages all members as equal partners in the process. | |
| 3 | Is possessive of the leadership role, making the organization dependent on him or her. Makes no room for others to succeed. Tries to contain the participation of new members. | Shares the leadership spotlight with others. Serves as a mentor and builds other leaders, thereby ensuring succession and continuity. Empowers members to excel. Recognizes contributions and achievements regularly. | |
| 4 | Is timid and hesitant to intervene. Is afraid of confrontation. Tries hard to please and doesn't know how to say no. Likes to be popular. | Intervenes proactively to reduce problems. Addresses dysfunctions with a principle-based approach. Is capable of saying no, gently but firmly, to ensure fairness for all and to facilitate effective decision making. | |
| 5 | Is impatient, egotistical, and short-tempered. Treats criticism or disagreements as personal attacks. Is condescending and disrespectful toward those who dare contradict him or her. | Is mature, patient, calm, reassuring, approachable, respectful, and supportive. Maintains freshness and a light touch. Is used to leaving his or her ego behind. | |

## Evaluating a Board Chair (continued)

| | Ineffective Board Chair<br>0 means *as bad as it gets* | Effective Board Chair<br>10 means *as good as it gets* | Score<br>0 to 10 |
|---|---|---|---|
| 6 | Is narrow-sighted, reactive, and crisis-driven. | Maintains a broad view of the issues. Is anchored in the Board's mission, vision, and strategy. Is planned and proactive. | |
| 7 | Is disorganized and unprepared for meetings. | Is organized, prepared, and knowledgeable. Acts like a role model and inspiration for others to follow. | |
| 8 | Is oblivious about and unconcerned with relationship building, both internally and externally. | Builds and maintains relationships with Board members, the CEO and staff, the community, external stakeholders, and suppliers. | |
| 9 | Has a poor sense of timing. Does not know when and how to bring closure to discussions and facilitate decision making. | Is intuitive and responsive to moods and needs at a meeting. Balances the need to make progress (time management) with the need for democratic and effective decision making. | |
| 10 | Is talkative and verbose. Offers rebuttals to every comment made by others. Is unable to facilitate a logical flow and step-by-step decision making or to summarize progress and initiate closure. | Communicates clearly, briefly, concisely, and logically. Is able to clarify decision-making options and divide multifaceted topics or decisions into manageable components. | |
| | GRAND TOTAL | Add the numbers in the righthand column.<br>(Minimum = 0.<br>Maximum = 100.) | |

# 5. EVALUATING A BOARD COLLECTIVELY

The table below can be used to evaluate your Board as a whole.

| | Ineffective Board<br>0 means *as bad as it gets* | Effective Board<br>10 means *as good as it gets* | Score<br>0 to 10 |
|---|---|---|---|
| 1 | Gets bogged down in small details. Micromanages the CEO and staff. Operates *on the ground floor* and does not attend to long-term goals. | Acts in a proactive, planned, sophisticated, and creative way. Is strategically focused, making room for the staff to excel. Operates *from the balcony*. | |
| 2 | Tolerates low commitment levels. Members are there because they *have* to be there, out of duty and obligation. They often miss meetings or fail to keep their promises. | Fosters genuine enthusiasm and commitment for the job. Members are there because they truly *want* to be there. They consistently keep their promises and deliver quality work. | |
| 3 | Accepts management's proposals without questioning. Embraces the status quo and blocks change. The opponents overpower the proponents. | Is conscientious and takes the time to carefully examine and scrutinize proposals. Questions the status quo and is open to new ideas. Benefits from both the critics and the creators. | |
| 4 | Fragmented. Is driven by narrow interests and personal agendas. Has a win-lose culture: *It's you against me.* Narrow majority decisions are common. Meetings feel like a combat zone. | Cohesive. Works as a team, while celebrating the diversity of talents and views. Has a win-win culture: *It's you and me against the problem.* Narrow majority decisions are rare. Meetings feel like a construction zone. | |
| 5 | Is impatient and shows little interest in learning or making informed decisions. Board members talk more than they listen. | Has an appetite for learning from members, staff, consultants, and the community. Board members listen more than they talk. | |

## Evaluating a Board Collectively (continued)

| | Ineffective Board<br>**0 means *as bad as it gets*** | Effective Board<br>**10 means *as good as it gets*** | Score<br>**0 to 10** |
|---|---|---|---|
| 6 | Builds dependencies on key leaders. Delegates duties without clear deliverables and deadlines. Works hard but isn't productive. | Constantly expands its leadership base. Delegates duties, with clear deliverables and deadlines, to officers, staff, and committees. Works smart and hard. | |
| 7 | Maintains a slow, monotonous, and boring pace. Performs routine, predictable, and menial work. | Keeps a dynamic and engaging pace, with exciting progress and quality decisions made. | |
| 8 | Allows dominant members to control agendas. Quieter members—together with their ideas, knowledge, and skills—are left behind. | Gives members equal opportunities to influence decisions, and provides them with the tools and knowledge to excel. Brings out the best in members and celebrates their successes. | |
| 9 | Provides unclear directions and poor leadership to the professional staff and does not demand excellence of them. | Provides thoughtful and credible directions to the professional staff. Fosters a staff culture that promotes and rewards excellence. | |
| 10 | Is arrogant and detached from the community and ignores its input, or capitulates to vocal minorities. | Is in touch and in tune with the community and listens to its input. Provides quality leadership and keeps the community informed. | |
| | **GRAND TOTAL** | Add the numbers in the righthand column. (Minimum = 0. Maximum = 100.) | |

# 6. EVALUATING A MEETING

The following table can be used to help you evaluate a meeting.

| | Ineffective Meeting<br>0 means *as bad as it gets* | Effective Meeting<br>10 means *as good as it gets* | Score<br>0 to 10 |
|---|---|---|---|
| 1 | There is only a weak connection between the meeting's agenda and the organization's mission, vision, and strategic goals. | There is a clear sense of purpose and a solid link between the agenda and the organization's mission, vision, and strategic goals. | |
| 2 | There is a haphazard, disorganized, and sometimes rushed decision-making process, with hasty solutions proposed to poorly defined problems and with no set criteria to evaluate solutions. | Problem solving is logical and organized, first defining the problem, then evaluating potential solutions (based on set criteria), then choosing the best option, and then assigning follow-up tasks. | |
| 3 | Members miss meetings, arrive late, leave early, are unprepared, answer cell phones during the meeting, and use high-tech devices to surf the Internet, pick up e-mails, or play games. | The right people arrive on time, are prepared fresh, equipped with the knowledge needed to make informed decisions, and committed to be there for the full meeting, in body and in spirit. | |
| 4 | Decisions are made and motions are voted on without any clarity as to the precise wording. Action items are vague or nonexistent. | There are clearly articulated consensus (or motions) and follow-up items. Concise minutes help ensure follow-up by capturing what was decided. | |

## Evaluating a Meeting (continued)

|   | Ineffective Meeting<br>0 means *as bad as it gets* | Effective Meeting<br>10 means *as good as it gets* | Score<br>0 to 10 |
|---|---|---|---|
| 5 | Vocal members dominate discussions and quiet members are left behind. | Participation is balanced. Every member has the same opportunity to influence decisions. Discussions are enriched by the diversity of views, insights, and ideas. | |
| 6 | Members do not speak up when a dysfunction occurs for fear of insulting others. They tolerate chaos, repetition, digressions, and personal attacks. | Members view themselves as partners in the decision-making process. They speak up if a dysfunction is damaging the quality of the decisions or the process itself. | |
| 7 | The meeting is slow and monotonous. Some people ramble and no one asks them to be brief. Some people fall asleep. Conversely, things move too quickly and people are afraid to raise concerns for fear of slowing the meeting down. | Time is well managed. The meeting's pace is dynamic and engaging but comfortable (not too fast and not too slow). Members speak concisely. More time is spent on significant issues, and less time is spent on minutiae. | |
| 8 | Rules for participation are not in place, leading to a sense of anarchy. Alternatively, rules are used too rigidly and stifle creativity and the free and natural flow of ideas, thereby making the meeting too formal and stuffy. | Essential rules are established: Wait to be recognized before speaking, stay on track, be brief and concise, etc. Rules are used flexibly so they do not stifle debate. The tone is kept humane, with an appropriate light touch. | |

## Evaluating a Meeting (continued)

| | Ineffective Meeting<br>0 means *as bad as it gets* | Effective Meeting<br>10 means *as good as it gets* | Score<br>0 to 10 |
|---|---|---|---|
| 9 | Personal attacks and insults are rampant. The climate is adversarial, with each faction using manipulative tactics to achieve its goals. | A courteous, respectful, and civilized tone is kept, even when issues are contentious. The focus is on issues and not personalities. The group works together toward common goals. | |
| 10 | The Board is distracted by logistical problems: a hot or cold room, outside noise, a faulty projector, catering issues, and so on. | Logistical details are handled flawlessly through meticulous planning and preparation and do not become a distraction. | |
| | **GRAND TOTAL** | Add the numbers in the righthand column.<br>(Minimum = 0.<br>Maximum = 100.) | |

# 7.  EVALUATING A CEO

The following table will help you evaluate your CEO.

| | Category | Score<br>0 to 10 |
|---|---|---|
| 1 | *Building Board capacity:* The CEO helps the Board optimize its effectiveness via a quality orientation program and via ongoing training and education. | |
| 2 | *Providing professional advice:* The CEO provides sound professional advice (with assistance from staff and external advisers) in a timely manner, helping the Board make balanced, legal, and sustainable decisions. | |

## Evaluating a CEO (continued)

| | Category | Score 0 to 10 |
|---|---|---|
| 3 | *Providing decision-making support:* The CEO provides analysis and decision-making options (possibly as written motions, circulated before meetings), reflecting Board policies and advancing strategic priorities. | |
| 4 | *Entrenching roles and responsibilities:* The CEO respects the Board's role to govern from the balcony (focusing on policy and strategy), while the CEO manages operations from the ground floor. The CEO shields staff from interference, harassment, and bullying by Board members. | |
| 5 | *Maintaining accountability:* The CEO reports regularly and proactively and provides full disclosure, in a manner that builds trust and reassures the Board that the organization is soundly managed, policies are adhered to, and strategic goals are advanced. | |
| 6 | *Risk management and dispute resolution:* The CEO detects risks and disputes at an early stage and addresses them in a proactive and timely manner. Staff members who wish to draw the Board's attention to significant issues are protected by whistle-blower policies. | |
| 7 | *Maintaining consistency, reliability, accessibility, and openness:* The CEO is consistent, reliable, and disciplined and displays an abundance of openness and accessibility. The lack of defensiveness makes it clear that there are no hidden problems or concealed risks. | |
| 8 | *Exchanging feedback with the Board:* The Board is assured that its feedback to the CEO is welcomed and responded to, and that conversely, it can count on the CEO's frank and principled feedback to help the Board achieve excellence in its governance practices. | |

## Evaluating a CEO (continued)

| | Category | Score 0 to 10 |
|---|---|---|
| 9 | *Optimizing staff performance:* The CEO hires effective staff members and ensures that they have the knowledge, skills, and motivation to excel in serving the organization. The CEO creates a safe and harassment-free environment, where staff members know that their input is valued and appreciated and never taken defensively. As a result, staff morale and retention are high and turnover is minimal. The CEO sets an example by optimizing his or her own performance and participating in relevant continuing education activities. | |
| 10 | *Building and maintaining relationships with the community:* The CEO ensures that community members and stakeholders are treated as valued partners and are greeted with courtesy and respect. This establishes satisfaction among citizens, shareholders, members, and stakeholders and boosts their loyalty to the organization. | |
| | **GRAND TOTAL** (Minimum = 0. Maximum = 100.) | |

# 8. EVALUATING A COMMUNITY

Effective and proactive Boards make efforts to learn about their communities and take initiatives to transform them into being more positive and engaged. Use the following form to evaluate your community.

| | Ineffective Community 0 means *as bad as it gets* | Effective Community 10 means *as good as it gets* | Score 0 to 10 |
|---|---|---|---|
| 1 | Community members look after their own interests and care less about other interests or the community as a whole. | Community members expect fairness and merit-based decisions. They place community interests ahead of personal ones. | |

## Evaluating a Community (continued)

| | Ineffective Community<br>0 means *as bad as it gets* | Effective Community<br>10 means *as good as it gets* | Score<br>0 to 10 |
|---|---|---|---|
| 2 | Community members readily criticize and find fault in others. The *politics of envy* means that it is not okay for someone else to succeed if you didn't. | Community members rejoice in the success of others, value excellence, and search for the good in others. | |
| 3 | There is apathy, acquiescence, and acceptance of mediocrity as a fact of life. | Community members demand excellence and principle-based leadership from their Board and refuse to tolerate dysfunctions. | |
| 4 | There is a culture of entitlement or dependency, where people expect things to be done for them. | There is a culture of self-reliance, where people are rewarded through their efforts. | |
| 5 | There is fear and hesitation to question authority, even when it is clear that leaders are taking excessive risks on behalf of the community. | Community members act as partners and co-owners. They routinely bring both cautions and positive ideas to their leaders' attention. | |
| 6 | There is instinctive suspicion of leaders. Innocent errors are judged as proof of incompetence, deliberate negligence, or even corruption. | People cautiously trust leaders while demanding transparency and accountability. Errors made in good faith are forgiven. | |
| 7 | There is fragmentation, adversity, and misery. | There is cohesion, collaboration, happiness, and pride in the community. | |
| 8 | There is a belief that leadership is about power and making backroom deals and promises. | There is intolerance of favoritism, nepotism, and corruption by leaders. | |

## Evaluating a Community (continued)

| | Ineffective Community<br>0 means *as bad as it gets* | Effective Community<br>10 means *as good as it gets* | Score<br>0 to 10 |
|---|---|---|---|
| 9 | There is a primary focus on status, money, prestige, and material possessions. | There is a holistic focus, expanded beyond status and material values, and into quality of life, environment, and community. | |
| 10 | There is impatience and a quest to get more things done and accumulate more things quickly. | There is patience and a focus on quality results, even if they take longer to achieve. | |
| | **GRAND TOTAL** | Add up the numbers in the righthand column.<br>(Minimum = 0.<br>Maximum = 100.) | |

<blockquote>
**A P P E N D I X  C**
</blockquote>

# MYTHS AND TRUTHS ABOUT RULES OF ORDER

The following table includes common myths and truths about parliamentary procedure. Keep in mind that if the statements below contradict your legislation, bylaws, or chosen book on parliamentary procedure, then the latter will have precedence in your organization and must be followed.

| Myth | Truth |
| --- | --- |
| The mover of a motion owns it in perpetuity. | The mover stops owning a motion once debate on it begins. From then on, the group owns it, and the mover no longer has the right to unilaterally withdraw or amend the motion. |

| Myth | Truth |
|---|---|
| A person must support a motion in order to second it. | By seconding a motion, a person indicates that the motion should be debated and not that he or she favors it. |
| If a motion is moved and seconded, it is automatically open for debate. | A motion is open for debate only after the Chair places it before the Board. The Chair may reject a motion on the grounds that it is in violation of a certain bylaw or rule, or he or she may delay it because it is poorly worded. |
| The Chair never votes except to break a tie. | Unless your legislation or bylaws say otherwise, the Board Chair, if present, may vote like other Board members. |
| A Board Chair is not allowed to speak in debate, unless he or she vacates the Chair. | Unless your legislation or bylaws say otherwise, the Chair of a small Board may speak in debate, but on the same basis as other members, i.e., by taking turns. |
| If a member *calls the question*, debate must cease. Calling the question may interrupt a person who is speaking and gets priority over anything else. | The decision to close debate is made by the group collectively and not unilaterally by the Chair or by one member. If a motion to close debate is made formally, it may not interrupt a person who is speaking, and its mover has no special priority in the speakers' lineup. |
| The mover may close debate by speaking on a motion a second time. | The mover does not have the right to unilaterally close debate unless your bylaws say so. |
| Minutes must include everything that was said at the meeting. | Minutes are primarily a record of what was done by the Board and not what was said by each member. |

| Myth | Truth |
|------|-------|
| A Board member may order that his or her opinions be entered in the minutes. | Minute takers should follow minute-taking standards, established by Board policy. They should not be subject to random demands by individual members. |
| There can be no debate until there is a motion on the floor. | The Board may opt to have informal discussion exploring the nature of a problem before introducing a motion. |

# APPENDIX D

# TOOLS FOR MEETING CHAIRS AND PARTICIPANTS

With the notion that *suffering is optional*, the table below provides sample scripts for meeting Chairs and participants so they can speak up if they encounter a problem during a meeting.

| If this occurs in a meeting: | You can say: |
|---|---|
| Digression | *"Sorry to interrupt, but can we please get back to the agenda?"* or *"How is this discussion related to the core issue, which is _____?"* |
| Rushing | *"Can we please slow down? I am not sure I understand what the proposal is or what the ramifications are. Can someone please clarify?"* |

| If this occurs in a meeting: | You can say: |
| --- | --- |
| Interruptions | *"Can we please wait to be recognized before we speak?"* <br> or <br> *"Can we please hear people out without interruption?"* |
| Last-minute motion | *"I am not comfortable debating a motion that is worded impromptu and without the benefit of professional expertise. I move that this motion be postponed until the next Board meeting."* <br> or <br> *"Given that it's late, I suggest that we only discuss this motion informally now and then refer it to our staff for study and professional analysis."* |
| Personal attacks | *"Point of order. We should be focusing on issues, not people."* <br> or <br> *"Can we please lower the tone of this conversation?"* |
| Micro-management | *"This discussion seems to be operational and more appropriate for staff than for the Board. It feels like we are on the ground floor. Can we please return to the balcony?"* |
| Rambling | *"Can we please keep our comments brief? I am concerned that we may run out of time for significant issues later on in the agenda."* <br> or <br> *"In the interests of time, can we please move on?"* |
| Repetition | *"Does anyone have anything new to add, and, if not, can we proceed to the vote?"* |
| Side conversation | *"I'm having trouble concentrating. Can we please have only one conversation at the same time?"* or <br> *"Tim and Connie. Is there a problem? We need you to focus on the discussion."* |

| If this occurs in a meeting: | You can say: |
|---|---|
| Domination | *"Can we hear from people who have not spoken?"*<br>or<br>*"Rick, I am curious. What do you think about this issue, given your expertise in financial planning?"* |
| Unclear motion | *"Can we please have the motion repeated?"*<br>or<br>*"Can we take a break so Robert and Judy can rewrite this motion? We need to be sure that we know what we're discussing and voting on. There is too much at stake here, and we cannot afford to be casual about it."* |

# INDEX

# ABOUT THE AUTHOR

**Eli Mina** is a board effectiveness consultant, executive coach, meeting mentor, and expert on rules of order. His practice is based in Vancouver, Canada. Since 1984, Eli has assisted his clients in managing contentious meetings, building better Boards and councils, preventing and dealing with disputes and dysfunctions, using rules of order sensibly and intelligently, and establishing minute-taking standards. Eli's clients come from municipal governments, school boards, credit unions, business and industry, native communities, regulatory bodies, and the nonprofit sector.

In addition to *101 Boardroom Problems and How to Solve Them*, Eli wrote *The Complete Handbook of Business Meetings, The Business Meetings Sourcebook, The Guide to Better Meetings for Directors of Non-Profit Organizations*, and *Mina's Guide to Minute Taking*. He holds bachelor's and master's degrees in engineering and completed a BC Justice Institute Conflict Resolution Certificate Program. He has the credentials of a Professional Registered Parliamentarian (PRP) and Certified Professional Parliamentarian (CPP).

Contact information for training programs and speaking engagements:

Phone: 604-730-0377

E-mail: eli@elimina.com

Website: www.elimina.com